Kindergarten
Readiness

Kindergarten
Readiness

Nancy L. Cappelloni

CORWIN
A SAGE Company

CORWIN
A SAGE Company

FOR INFORMATION:

Corwin
A SAGE Company
2455 Teller Road
Thousand Oaks, California 91320
(800) 233-9936
www.corwin.com

SAGE Publications Ltd.
1 Oliver's Yard
55 City Road
London EC1Y 1SP
United Kingdom

SAGE Publications India Pvt. Ltd.
B 1/I 1 Mohan Cooperative Industrial Area
Mathura Road, New Delhi 110 044
India

SAGE Publications Asia-Pacific Pte. Ltd.
3 Church Street
#10-04 Samsung Hub
Singapore 049483

Acquisitions Editor: Jessica Allan
Editorial Assistant: Lisa Whitney
Production Editor: Cassandra Margaret Seibel
Copy Editor: Erin Livingston
Typesetter: C&M Digitals (P) Ltd.
Proofreader: Caryne Brown
Indexer: Jean Casalegno
Cover Designer: Karine Hovsepian
Permissions Editor: Karen Ehrmann

Printed in the United States of America.

Library of Congress Cataloging-in-Publication Data

Cappelloni, Nancy.

Kindergarten readiness / Nancy L. Cappelloni.

p. cm.
Includes bibliographical references and index.

ISBN 978-1-4522-4194-4 (pbk.)

1. Readiness for school—United States.
2. Kindergarten—United States. 3. Kindergarten—Curricula—United States. I. Title.

LB1132.C36 2013
372.21'8—dc23   2012020440

This book is printed on acid-free paper.

SUSTAINABLE FORESTRY INITIATIVE
Certified Chain of Custody
Promoting Sustainable Forestry
www.sfiprogram.org
SFI-01268
SFI label applies to text stock

12 13 14 15 16 10 9 8 7 6 5 4 3 2 1

Contents

Figures, Tables, and Resources

Dedication

This book is dedicated to my three beautiful daughters—Lauren, Lisa, and Dana—for their unconditional love, for providing me with the joy of parenting, and for teaching me firsthand how children learn, flourish, and grow. I thank my husband, Robert, for his love, understanding, and encouragement.

I would also like to dedicate this book to all the early childhood educators and kindergarten teachers in this country, who tirelessly nurture young children and impassion them with the gift of knowledge.

Finally, this book is dedicated to the hundreds of kindergarten students I have had the pleasure of teaching. Being a kindergarten teacher has not only provided me with the knowledge of how children learn and develop but has filled my life with wonder, purpose, and laughter. Thank you for having me as your teacher and for all that *you* have taught *me*. I hope that I have inspired in you the love of learning and the realization that you can be and do all that you aspire to.

Chad, Tjai, John, Olivia, Molly, Liam, Maxwell, David, Trudie, Patrick, Andrew, Sara, Katie, Laura, Julia, Emily, Willie, Madalyn, Victor, Stephen, Jason, Mackenzie, Sophie, Grace, Laura, Haley, Chet, Erika, Kyle, Benjamin, Gabrielle, Landon, Ellie, Tyler, Christian, Henry, Monica, Cameron, Patrick, Lena, McKenzie, Matthew, Tyler, Savannah, Sabrina, Thomas, Sophia, Kiara, Catherine, Max, Nicholas, Vincent, Sophia, Charlotte, Madeline, Luc, Andrew, Jackson, Javid, Grant, Nataya, Kade, Jenna, Isabella, Anna, Jonathan, Lauren, Phoebe, Collin, Arianna, Elliot, Sarah, Lucas, Emily, Katherine, Damien, Melissa, Spencer, Olivia, Nicolas, Margot, Conner, Sarah, Bridget, Cassidy, Dillon, Alex, Zev, Mitchel, Justin, Ryan, Madeline, Theo, Simonne, William, Zoe, Roman, Jack, Cole, Dylan, Shayna, Casey, James, Camille, Graham, Matthew, Chace, Miranda, Morgan, Ariana, Nesibe, Molly, Natalie, Kira, Lauren, Theo, Kylie, Zoe, Jacob, Eric, Ruby, Dorothy, Laurence, Samuel, Colin, Isaac, Elisabeth, Alexandra, Julien, Xena, Marina,

Aristotle, William, Brooks, Nikoline, Monica, Mary, Jennifer, Katarina, Sabrina, Brian, Duncan, Erick, Devon, Mia, Teymour, Nicolas, Paige, Lucy, Gregory, Cameron, Katie, Samantha, Roy, Victoria, Shiva, Jake, Gianni, Scott, Ashley, Sydney, Jack, Henry, Tahir, Zoe, Julia, Elana, Ian, Lyla, Charlie, Keiler, Tessa, Blake, Lauren, Carolina, Francesca, Mateo, Nikki, Sarah, Christopher, Cooper, Parker, Fiona, Jak, Jacob, John, Aliza, Maxwell, Aneese, Augustine, Brooke, Ben, Carlyn, D'Andre, Dean, Evan, John-Davis, Benny, Lane, Max, Nicole, Sam, Skylar, Tristan, Paco, Robert, Ruby, Jacob, Jackson, Matheus, Margaret, Sa'ar, Makena, Thomas, Christopher, Sydney, Kelly, Jim, Zoe, Nate, Sofia, Jack, Oliver, John, Pearse, Reece, Wyatt, Mia, Will, Hank, Julian, Logan, Liam, Lily, Maizy, Addison, Jayden, Ryan, Kate, Kristin, William, Finn, Riley, Emily, Erica, Laurent, Charlie, Harrison, Ava, Robert, Tate, Jack, Caiden, Riaan, Belinda, Ben, Cole, Savia, Andie, Jackson, Sophie, Petra, Graham, Adam, Ellie, Finn, Matthew, Johnny, Leila, Addie, Leo, Antonio, Grady, Livvy, Charlotte, Griffin, Dara, and Santiago.

About the Author

 **Nancy L. Cappelloni**, EdD, is an educational consultant and adjunct professor in the Teacher Education Department in the University of San Francisco's School of Education. She has taught kindergarten and early childhood education for the past twenty years. Dr. Cappelloni consults privately with families and their young children, helping them navigate through the processes of readiness for and the transition to kindergarten. She also works with elementary-age children experiencing a wide range of learning challenges. Dr. Cappelloni works collaboratively with the child's family, school, and other specialists to create an integrative intervention system and partnership to optimize the child's social and academic success in school.

Dr. Cappelloni is a member of the board of directors in the California Kindergarten Association (CKA) and serves on the Transitional Kindergarten Task Force. She is a member of a number of professional organizations, including the National Association for the Education of Young Children (NAEYC), the California Association for the Education of Young Children (CAEYC), the International Reading Association (IRA), Phi Delta Kappa International (PDK), the Association for Supervision and Curriculum Development (ASCD), and the American Educational Research Association (AERA).

Dr. Cappelloni holds a doctorate in education, a California Multiple Subject Teaching Credential/Cross-Cultural Language and Academic Development (CLAD) certificate, and a California Early Childhood Education Administrative Credential. She conducts numerous professional development workshops for early childhood educators and primary school teaching staff on topics including kindergarten readiness, readiness assessments, emergent literacy, and self-regulated learning. Additionally, Dr. Cappelloni presents family workshops on kindergarten readiness and directs kindergarten readiness programs throughout the year.

Dr. Cappelloni coauthored Corwin's *The New Elementary Teacher's Handbook* (3rd edition, 2011) and is the author of two cookbooks, *Ethnic Cooking the Microwave Way* (1994) and *Cranberry Cooking for All Seasons* (2002). More information about Dr. Nancy Cappelloni can be found at http://cappellonilearning.com or by e-mailing nrlcapp@gmail.com.

Introduction

Entering school ready to learn has become a growing concern in this country. Over three-and-one-half million children enter the nation's public kindergartens each year, and an additional one-half million enter private schools each year (National Center for Education Statistics, 2012). Children begin school with considerable variation in their range of general knowledge, skills, and abilities. Entering kindergartners come from increasingly diverse ethnic, racial, cultural, social, economic, and language backgrounds, and they differ enormously in their early care and educational experiences prior to kindergarten.

Many families are concerned with whether their children will have the knowledge and skills at age five to succeed in kindergarten. Many early childhood educators are fearful that developmental, play-based preschools may not be preparing children for the rigors they will face upon kindergarten entry. Kindergarten teachers report that many children enter school unprepared for the challenges and the transition to kindergarten, and they express concerns that many children are not optimally ready to learn, putting them at risk for school failure, retention, or in need of later intervention.

The kindergarten year has clearly been shown to have important consequences for a child's acquisition of knowledge and skills that are powerful determinants for later school success (Pianta & Cox, 1999). Readiness skills at the beginning of kindergarten are associated with educational outcomes in later years. From the start of kindergarten, children considered to be at risk of school failure start behind, lag behind, and stay behind. More important, early school problems generally persist and intensify as well as predict school adjustment and later academic problems, including retention, dropout, incidences of delinquency, and even aggression, crime, and violence (Boyd, Barnett, Bodrova, Leong, & Gomby, 2005; Fantuzzo, King, & Heller, 1992; Princiotta, Flanagan, & Germino Hausken, 2006; Tremblay, Gervais, & Petitclerc, 2008).

The acquisition of a child's readiness skills and children's success in school can be traced back to and are associated with multiple factors and early childhood educational experiences in preschool, family characteristics, and influences during the years prior to kindergarten (Shonkoff & Phillips, 2000; West, Denton, & Germino Hausken, 2000; Zill & West, 2001). Recent advances in developmental neuroscience provide greater insight into early brain development, revealing that the first five years in a child's life are a time of extraordinary development. Young children have an impressive learning capacity during these critical years before kindergarten.

Learning and development during the early years occur in all areas, or *domains,* of a young child's development—physical/motor development; social and emotional development; approaches toward learning; language and communication development; emerging literacy development; and cognitive development and general knowledge (Copple & Bredekamp, 2009; Kagan, Moore, & Bredekamp, 1995; Shonkoff & Phillips, 2000; Thompson, 2008). These domains are associated with and often are predictors of children's success in kindergarten and later school years, and they do not operate in isolation from one another (Bowman, Donovan, & Burns, 2001; Boyd et al., 2005; LaParo & Pianta, 2000; Shonkoff & Phillips, 2000; Strickland & Riley-Ayers, 2006; Thompson, 2008). The nurturing of all these domains during the preschool years is essential both for children's early learning and for children's educational achievements in following years.

Little attention was paid to the issue of school readiness prior to the 1990s. Children in the United States entered school with great discrepancies in skills, family backgrounds, and early educational experiences. Individual and cultural variations in children were often mistaken for a demonstration of their deficiencies, rather than differences, in their school readiness (Kagan et al., 1995). Today, there is a heightened sense of urgency regarding children's readiness for school. The National Association for the Education of Young Children (NAEYC) asserts that any discussion of school readiness must consider the following three factors: (1) the diversity and inequity of children's early life experiences, (2) the wide variation in young children's development and learning, and (3) the degree to which school expectations of children entering kindergarten are reasonable, appropriate, and supportive of individual differences (NAEYC & National Association of Early Childhood Specialists in State Departments of Education, 2002).

Recent research has shown that children's kindergarten readiness skills can be significantly enhanced through effective preschool programs. The following chapters of this book will not only help educators understand the complexity of kindergarten readiness but will also lay a foundation on which to implement a high-quality, developmentally appropriate curriculum that encourages growth and development in *all* children's readiness for school.

DEFINITION OF KEY TERMS

The following terms have been defined for the purpose of this book:

1. *At risk for school failure:* The term refers to factors associated with lower performance on measures of academic achievement. Children are often designated as *at-risk* when they possess two or more of the following risk factors: children have a non-English primary language in the home, children live in a single-parent family, children's mothers have less than a high school education, and children's families receive welfare assistance (West, Denton, & Reaney, 2001).

2. *Early childhood education experiences:* participation in preschool, nursery school, prekindergarten, Head Start, or a child care center prior to kindergarten.

3. *Early learning standards:* developmentally appropriate early childhood standards and performance expectations for preschool children's learning and development. Content is implemented through informed practice in the following five domains identified in the National Education Goals Panel (NEGP) documents: (1) physical and motor, (2) social and emotional, (3) approaches toward learning, (4) language and communication, and (5) cognition and general knowledge.

4. *High-quality preschool:* a preschool program with a high rating in the following areas: child-teacher interactions, activities, materials, learning opportunities, health and safety routines, classroom environment, adult-child ratio, relationships with families, and the education and training of teachers and staff.

5. *Kindergarten readiness:* a multidimensional view of the attributes that preschool-age children demonstrate at the time of kindergarten entry. These attributes or characteristics fall within seven domains of early learning and development: (1) physical well-being and motor development, (2) social development, (3) emotional development, (4) approaches toward learning, (5) language and communication development, (6) emergent literacy, and (7) cognitive development and general knowledge.

6. *Kindergarten readiness skills:* specific skills, abilities, and characteristics that preschool-age children demonstrate at the time of kindergarten entry.

7. *Preschool-age children* or *preschoolers:* all children between the ages of three to five. This includes children in prekindergarten programs.

8. *Prekindergarten:* any type of publicly funded or private preschool program for children between the ages of four and six preceding kindergarten entry.

9. *Transition:* The transition process is the period of time beginning the year before kindergarten entrance and continuing through the kindergarten year (Pianta, Cox, Taylor, & Early, 1999).

PROFESSIONAL DEVELOPMENT DISCUSSION GUIDE

The purpose of the professional development discussion guide at the end of each chapter is

- to provide meaningful inquiry topics and relevant questions for thinking, discussing, clarifying, and helping to develop a common understanding.
- to help create a system for continuous dialogue, communication, and the exchange of ideas.
- to help make connections from theory to practical early childhood application.
- to help improve and sustain professional practice.
- to help build a collaborative culture in the early childhood educational setting.

Source: Reprinted with permission of Phi Delta Kappa International, www.pdkintl.org. All rights reserved.

1

Conceptualizing Kindergarten Readiness

What Does It Mean to Be Ready for Kindergarten?

Within the past two decades, an increased interest in kindergarten readiness has emerged alongside a growing body of research literature. Researchers, practitioners, and policymakers have attempted to provide greater understanding of this complex phenomenon. Conceptualizing kindergarten readiness has been, and remains, a challenging and often controversial task.

Conceptualizations of school readiness have been influenced by varying and often different perspectives. The complexity of kindergarten readiness becomes more apparent as one tries to establish operational definitions, guidelines, standards, articulations, and timelines. Earlier conceptualizations of readiness suggest that readiness is fixed—determined by specific indicators such as age, ability, or maturation. Other perspectives defined readiness as the acquisition of a certain set of prerequisite skills or proficiencies. Later models assert that readiness is developmental and comprises interrelated factors. One of these models conceptualized school readiness as comprising the social, political, organizational, educational, and personal resources that support the child's success at school entry. This model takes into account the shared responsibilities that families, communities, and schools have in providing nurturing environments that promote children's learning (Piotrkowski, Botsko, & Matthews, 2000).

The Early Childhood Longitudinal Study, Kindergarten Class of 1998–99 (ECLS-K) sponsored by the U.S. Department of Education, National Center for Education Statistics (NCES), conducted a large-scale national study examining kindergartners and their schools, classrooms, teachers, and families. A nationally representative sample of 22,782 kindergartners was followed through their eighth grade year (Princiotta, Flanagan, & Germino Hausken, 2006; Walston, Rathbun, & Germino Hausken, 2008; West, Denton, & Germino Hausken, 2000). The children in the study were enrolled in a total of 1,277 public, private, full-day, and half-day kindergarten programs. The sample included children from diverse racial, ethnic, and socioeconomic backgrounds. Assessments were designed to measure children's early academic skills, physical growth, fine and gross motor development, health, social skills, problem behavior, and approaches to learning (Snyder, Dillow, & Hoffman, 2008; West et al., 2000; Zill & West, 2001).

The ECLS-K study associated poor educational outcomes (such as low achievement/test scores, retention, suspension or expulsion, and dropping out of school) with four risk factors (Zill & West, 2001): low maternal education (having a mother who has less than a high school education); living in a welfare-dependent family; living in a single-parent home; and having parents whose primary language was one other than English. Findings indicated that 46 percent of all four-year-olds who had not yet entered kindergarten had at least one of these risk factors; 31 percent of these children had two or more risk factors; and 16 percent had three or more. Risk factors were found to be more common among kindergartners from racial/ethnic minorities than among those from white families. Nearly half of those children identified with multiple risk factors scored in the bottom quartile in reading, math, and general knowledge skills. Risk factors were associated not only with children's lower literacy and math skills but with problem behaviors that affect peer interactions and with a lack of task persistence, eagerness to learn, and attention (West, Denton, & Reaney, 2001). Further research indicates that children's cognitive skills and knowledge at the beginning of kindergarten have been shown to be associated with gains in reading and math in later grades and to predict later reading and math achievement (Denton & West, 2002; McClelland, Acock, & Morrison, 2006). Overall, children who fall behind in kindergarten are still behind in fifth and eighth grade (Princiotta et al., 2006; Walston, Rathbun, & Germino Hausken, 2008).

Concerns that many children from disadvantaged families are insufficiently prepared to begin formal schooling has motivated a greater focus on the importance of early childhood education and readiness for kindergarten. Data from the National Center for Children in Poverty (NCCP) indicates that the proportion of young children living in low-income families is rising. There are more than 72 million children living in the United States under the age of 18, and 65 percent of them live in either low-income or poor families. In 2010, 48 percent of children ages three through five—or almost six million—lived in low-income families (NCCP, 2012). On average, four-year-olds living in poverty have been shown to be about 18 months behind developmentally compared to what is typical for others in their age group. This developmental lag between children from low-income and middle-class families is particularly alarming because it contributes to an achievement gap that persists into kindergarten and far beyond (Copple & Bredekamp, 2009).

Common Core Standards and State Content Standards for kindergarten, which describe what children are expected to learn and be able to do by the end of kindergarten, have become increasingly demanding. The accelerated academic standards and growing expectations for kindergarten students to meet Common Core Standards and State Content Standards demand greater preparedness from children in the years prior to kindergarten entry. Many educators believe that the current kindergarten curriculum resembles what used to be taught in the first grade. There is growing concern about depriving children of play in their early school years by driving them too hard academically. Concerns that children entering kindergarten are unprepared for the challenges that lie ahead, due in large part to the concern that many children enter school already at risk of failure, have led to an increased interest in kindergarten readiness.

The growing evidence that early childhood experiences are intricately linked to later school success has fueled recent interest in the importance of making sure all children entering kindergarten are ready to learn. Recent research indicates that a high-quality preschool experience is associated with academic achievement in kindergarten and has long-term social and emotional outcomes. Preschool has been shown to benefit all children and prepare them for the transition to the accelerated academic demands of kindergarten (Barnett, Epstein, Friedman, Boyd, & Hustedt, 2008; Barnett & Yarosz, 2007; Head Start Bureau, 2005; Magnuson, Ruhm, & Waldfogel, 2007; Marcon, 2002).

In order to renew a federal commitment to improving educational achievement and increasing the country's commitment to students, teachers, and schools, President George H.W. Bush and the 50 state governors established the first National Education Goal in 1989. *Goal One,* referred to as the *Readiness Goal,* stated that by the year 2000, all children in America would start school ready to learn. Although the National Education Goals Panel (NEGP) Report on Goal One did not use the word *readiness* (NEGP, 1993), this goal was instrumental in the development of a common language about preparedness for kindergarten and was pivotal in the recognition that all children in this country should start school ready to learn.

Recognizing the wide range of abilities and experiences that influence early learning and development, the NEGP suggested that a child's performance encompasses a wide range of abilities, skills, and individual characteristics. The NEGP's Resource and Technical Planning Groups (Kagan, Moore, & Bredekamp, 1995) drew upon the research in early childhood education indicating that early learning and development are embedded within five interrelated dimensions: physical and motor development, social and emotional development, approaches toward learning, language development, and cognitive development and general knowledge. The NEGP established a multidimensional framework in which to conceptualize readiness, recognizing the interconnectedness of these five domains of early development and learning.

The NEGP multidimensional model of kindergarten readiness, perceived by many as the closest approximation to a national consensus on areas of early learning and development (Scott-Little, Kagan, & Frelow, 2005), articulated that school readiness does not comprise of a single set of skills or proficiencies but a range of variables and proficiencies in different developmental domains, each empirically linked with later success in school (Kagan et al., 1995). School readiness is viewed as a multifaceted construct in which the interconnectedness of many factors impacts a child's early learning and development. These include the individual characteristics of the child, the child's family, the cultural and contextual variability in each child's early learning and development, and early childhood education programs, schools, and teachers to support children's early learning, development, and competencies (Kagan et al., 1995).

The NEGP established a new model for school readiness by acknowledging that readiness is a collaborative process influenced by many interrelated factors. It established three objectives, suggesting that these critical components interact with and impact a child's learning, development, and readiness for school, and that they are associated with later school success: (1) the availability of a high-quality, developmentally appropriate preschool program; (2) parent participation and support in the child's education; and (3) the child's physical and mental health (Kagan et al., 1995; West et al., 2001).

The NEGP recognized that readiness requires not only prepared children but also the capacity and readiness of the nation's schools to be responsive to *all* children entering kindergarten. In the report, *Ready Schools* (Shore, 1998), the NEGP suggested that policies and strategies be either introduced or expanded to create learning climates optimal for all children. The particular skills, abilities, and knowledge that children bring to kindergarten are not only a function of their experiences prior to kindergarten but are impacted by the "readiness" of the school in which they enroll and the smooth transition between home, early care, preschool, and kindergarten (Kagan et al., 1995; National Association for the Education of Young Children and National Association of Early Childhood Specialists in State Departments of Education (NAEYC & NAECS/SDE), 2002; NEGP, 1993; Shore, 1998).

CONCLUSION

The NEGP framework, grounded in empirical research in early development and learning, was instrumental in the development of a common conceptualization of readiness, and it helped provide a national framework for education reform intended to ensure equitable educational opportunities and high levels of educational achievement for all students. The NEGP helped define, articulate, and clarify the domains of early learning and development that impact children's readiness for school, recognizing that a child's early learning experiences are associated with later success in school (Kagan et al., 1995; West et al., 2001) and established the foundation for many states' early learning standards in early childhood education. The NEGP framework provides the foundation for this book and the articulation of children's readiness for school.

Figure 1.1 Readiness for School: A Multidimensional Framework

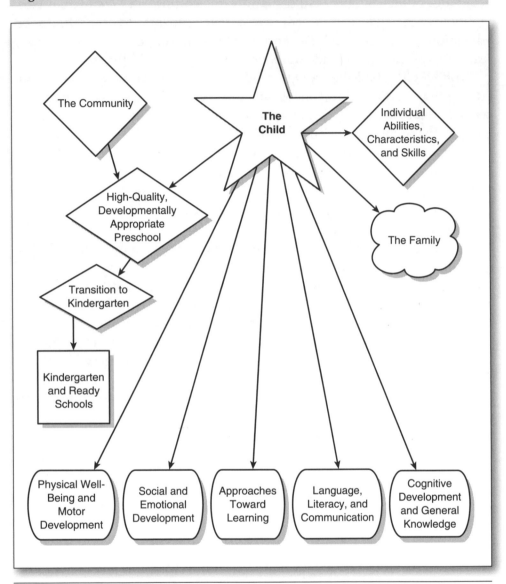

Source: Adapted from the National Education Goals Panel, 1995; Cappelloni, 2010.

PROFESSIONAL DEVELOPMENT DISCUSSION GUIDE

1. Deepen Your Thinking:

    a. Choose one or more of these individual inquiry topics for group discussion

        i. What factors impact a child's readiness for school?

        ii. What components contribute to a child's readiness besides the characteristics of the individual child?

iii. What are the possible consequences for children beginning school at risk for failure and possibly not being successful in kindergarten?

iv. What has contributed to recent concerns about kindergarten readiness?

WHERE CAN I LEARN MORE?

California Department of Education http://www.cde.ca.gov/index.asp

National Association for the Education of Young Children (NAEYC) http://www.naeyc.org

National Center for Children in Poverty (NCCP) http://www.nccp.org

National Center for Education Statistics (NCES) http://nces.ed.gov/

National Institute for Early Education Research (NIEER) http://nierr.org

United States Department of Education http://www.ed.gov

2

A New Framework for Kindergarten Readiness

T he framework of early learning and development recognized by the National Education Goal Panel (NEGP) articulated that school readiness is a multifaceted construct incorporating the interrelatedness of families, early childhood education programs, schools, teachers, and the broader community that supports children's early success in school. Further, this NEGP framework suggested that school readiness comprises a wide range of variables encompassing five interconnected and interrelated domains: (1) physical well-being and motor development, (2) social and emotional development, (3) approaches toward learning, (4) language development, and (5) cognitive development and general knowledge. Development in one domain often influences and/or is contingent on development in other domains (Kagan, Moore, & Bredekamp, 1995).

In order to further differentiate the domains and articulate the curricular goals and objectives for each comprehensively, the five original domains of early learning and development as designed in NEGP's framework have been expanded into seven domains by Cappelloni (2010). This was done by separating social and emotional development into two constructs—social development and emotional development—and by separating language development into two constructs—language and communication development and emerging literacy development. This was done for a number of reasons. Research over the past 20 years has indicated that kindergarten teachers place a strong emphasis on both the social and emotional characteristics of readiness (Cappelloni, 2010; Hains, Fowler, Schwartz, Kottwitz, & Rosenkoetter, 1989; Heaviside & Farris, 1993; Lin, Lawrence, & Gorrell, 2003; Piotrkowski, Botsko, & Matthews, 2000; Wesley & Buysse, 2003); therefore, it was determined that these two domains should be separated. Given that states' preschool early learning standards are heavily weighted in activities promoting language development and emerging literacy, it was also determined to separate the language development domain into two separate domains. Figure 2.1 demonstrates this revised, comprehensive model for kindergarten readiness. A description of the seven domains follows.

PHYSICAL WELL-BEING AND MOTOR DEVELOPMENT

The domain of physical well-being and motor development encompass the characteristics, skills, and abilities of a child's physical health and overall well-being; self-help skills; fitness; and gross motor, fine motor, graphomotor, and sensorimotor abilities. Children's health has been directly linked to school performance. It has been shown to have a direct impact on student behavior, peer interactions, and classroom management. Whereas healthy children are able to focus on and actively engage in experiences crucial for learning, health problems can interfere with learning, can create both social and academic barriers in kindergarten, and may prevent a successful start in kindergarten. For example, regular physical activity can help build and maintain healthy bodies, reduce feelings of depression and anxiety, and increase a child's capacity for learning. Developing motor skills can contribute to a child's sense of attaining new goals and improve cooperation with peers. Poor fitness can result in reduced energy and prevents children from participating in group activities (Copple & Bredekamp, 2009; Kagan, et al., 1995).

The following are key attributes of physical well-being and motor development:

- Gross motor skills
- Spatial awareness
- Body awareness
- Fine motor skills
  - o Use of scissors, glue stick, paintbrush, Legos, sewing cards, hole punch, and other small manipulatives
- Graphomotor (writing) skills
  - o Pencil grip; tracing and copying shapes, numbers, or letters; coloring within lines; drawing a person; writing own name
- Self-help skills
  - o Caring for self; dressing; eating; cleaning up
- Overall health, fitness, and stamina
  - o Adequate nutrition and sleep
- Mental alertness

SOCIAL DEVELOPMENT

A strong body of research links children's social competence with school readiness and overall academic achievement during kindergarten as well as later in life. The domain of social development encompasses the characteristics, skills, and abilities that enable children to have positive, secure, and successful interactions and relationships with others, including peers, teachers, and other adults. It has been found that many students enter kindergarten without sufficient social skills and/or the behavioral readiness necessary to participate in learning activities leading to academic success.

Research in neuroscience suggests that interactions with responsive social partners have tremendous impact on the growing brain. The early childhood years are a pivotal time for establishing and nurturing the development of relationships with other children. Peer relationships contribute to children's long-term social development (Kemple, David, & Hysmith, 1997; Shonkoff & Phillips, 2000). Positive interactions and relationships between teachers and children in early childhood educational settings impact the child's early experiences in academic, social, and emotional domains; they are critical for the development of the child's early learning experiences; and they promote more optimal achievement (Domitrovich, Gest, Gill, Bierman, Welsh, & Jones, 2009; Neuman & Cunningham, 2009; Perry & VandeKamp, 2000; Perry, VandeKamp, Mercer, & Nordby, 2002). Children's relationships with their teachers in early child care settings have also been shown to be important predictors not only of their social relations with peers and their behavior in general but also of school achievement in later years (Shonkoff & Phillips, 2000). Teachers who maintain interactions with young children and are responsive and sensitive to their needs can provide stimulation that is calibrated to the child's readiness for new learning (Thompson, 2008). Young children who feel supported and accepted by adults and who have positive and secure adult attachments are also likely to have higher self-esteem (Copple & Bredekamp, 2009). Since the amount of adult-child interaction time in many families is shrinking, due in part to single-parent and dual-income families, the teacher-child relationship is particularly important for both academic and developmental outcomes (Christenson, 1999).

The following indicators are key attributes of social development:

- Interactions (social skills) and relationships with peers
- Interactions (social skills) and relationships with teachers and adults
- Respect and caring for others
- Forming and maintaining new friendships with peers
- Cooperating and playing with other children
- Cooperating with teachers
- Understanding feelings of others
- Resolving conflict through compromise and negotiation
- Sharing and taking turns
- Following directions

EMOTIONAL DEVELOPMENT

The domain of emotional development encompasses the characteristics, skills, and abilities that enable children to both have positive feelings about themselves and demonstrate self-control in the classroom setting. The preschool child's developing competencies are necessary for the child to manage emotions, handle stress, inhibit behavior, and focus attention on important tasks. A child's emotional self-regulation has strong implications for the fostering of positive peer relationships and interactions (Shonkoff & Phillips, 2000). The following are key attributes of emotional development in the classroom:

- Sense of personal well-being
- Positive self-concept
- Self-control
- Self-awareness
- Self-regulation of emotions
- Self-efficacy
- Self-confidence and pride
- Expression of emotions and feelings
- Sensitivity and empathy towards others
- Acceptance of others' differences
- Respecting the rights of others/staying in own space
- Understanding the impact of one's own behavior
- Understanding the consequences of one's behavior
- Separating from parent easily

APPROACHES TOWARD LEARNING

The domain of approaches toward learning encompasses the inclinations, dispositions, and styles reflective of the ways children become engaged in learning and approach learning tasks. Learning-related skills and higher levels of behavioral self-regulation in kindergarten are associated with higher academic achievement. Behavioral regulation involves multiple components of executive functioning: attentional focusing, working memory, and inhibitory control. Proficiency in behavioral aspects of self-regulation, through teacher support and specific instructional practices, helps children adjust to school, helps them in their social interactions, and enables them to become more independent, academically effective learners. Research has demonstrated that poorly self-regulated children are at greater risk of low achievement, emotional and behavioral problems, and even school dropout (Ponitz, McClelland, Matthews, & Morrison; 2009). The following indicators have been identified as key attributes of development in approaches toward learning:

- Independence
- Interest and enthusiasm in learning
- Curiosity, imagination, and invention
- Eagerness and engagement in new tasks
- Accepting new challenges
- Initiative, effort, and task persistence
- Attentiveness
- Concentration and focus
- Transitioning from one activity to the next
- Problem solving
- Following routines
- Following classroom rules and directions
- Positive orientation towards school

LANGUAGE AND COMMUNICATION DEVELOPMENT

The domain of language and communication development encompasses the characteristics, skills, and abilities that enable children to express themselves and communicate with others. The exposure to and acquisition of language and communicative competence provides the foundation for successful social interactions and provides the foundation for all curricula throughout school—a necessity for academic success in all subject areas (Copple & Bredekamp, 2009).

Vocabulary development during the child's first three years of life has been shown to significantly impact kindergarten literacy skills. Young children exposed to language-rich environments have the benefit of exposure to vocabulary development through interactions with books, all forms of print, and rich conversations. Children with larger vocabularies become more proficient readers, have greater reading comprehension and read more widely, and have higher academic gains (Lubliner & Smetana, 2005) than those with limited vocabularies. Hart and Risley (1995, 2003) observed that children from low-income families have significantly more limited experience with language, particularly in vocabulary development, than children from middle-income families. By age three, significant disparities exist in children's vocabulary that have substantial associations with language development and school success. Children with limited vocabulary lag behind in kindergarten, exhibit lower reading abilities, are often resistant to reading, maintain smaller vocabularies, and often stay behind as they progress through school and into adulthood. Children begin kindergarten with large discrepancies in their language and literacy knowledge and skills. Catching up is difficult for "vocabulary-disadvantaged children" (Biemiller, 2003 p. 3), and gaining these skills would require these children to acquire new vocabulary at above-average rates. These vocabulary limitations are a major component in the achievement gap (Biemiller, 2001; Hart & Risley, 1995, 2003; Lubliner & Smetana, 2005; Shonkoff & Phillips, 2000; Snow, Burns, & Griffin, 1998).

The following indicators have been identified as key attributes of language and communication development:

- Receptive language abilities (listening skills)
  - Attentive listening
  - Following directions
  - Comprehension
- Expressive language abilities (speaking skills)
  - Vocabulary and word meaning
  - Language mechanics
  - English language proficiency
  - Communication
  - Asking and answering questions
  - Engaging in conversation
  - Singing and reciting nursery rhymes

EMERGING LITERACY DEVELOPMENT

Research on literacy development suggests that the processes of reading, writing, speaking, listening, and thinking develop simultaneously as learners become literate (Shonkoff & Phillips, 2000). Early literacy experiences in preschool have strong links to long-lasting reading successes in school. The National Institute for Literacy (2009) reported that the strongest and most consistent predictors of later literacy development include preschool emergent literacy skills, such as alphabet knowledge, phonological awareness, and writing letters. These skills, particularly letter knowledge and phonological awareness, were found to have predictive significance for later reading, confirming the link between emergent literacy in preschool with later reading ability in primary school (Lonigan, Burgess, & Anthony, 2000).

The following indicators have been identified as key attributes of emerging literacy development:

- Phonemic and phonological awareness
- Alphabetic knowledge
- Concepts of print
- Recognizing environmental print (signs, labels, etc.)
- Book awareness and book handling
  - Looking at books
  - Understanding that books have meaning
- Story sense
  - Retelling a familiar story
  - Sequencing a familiar story
  - Story comprehension
- Writing
  - Writing letters of the alphabet
  - Writing name
  - Communicating through writing and drawing

COGNITIVE DEVELOPMENT AND GENERAL KNOWLEDGE

The domain of cognitive development and general knowledge encompasses indicators measuring the knowledge base a child has and the child's ability to represent the world cognitively within three types of knowledge—physical knowledge, logico-mathematical knowledge, and social-conventional knowledge. A foundation comprising factual knowledge, skills, and conceptual understandings of information has been found to promote cognitive development and general knowledge.

Play has important benefits for young children's cognitive growth. Play provides opportunities for children to discover, explore, invent, experiment, question, construct, and assimilate new knowledge. In fact, research studies have indicated that play is an important activity for children to informally learn important skills. In one study, four-year-old children from 10 different countries who spent time in child care and educational settings that encouraged free choice activities, had a wide range of materials available, and provided opportunities to explore materials and solve problems were *all* found to have more significant gains in their cognitive performance at age seven than children in settings lacking those qualities (Montie, Xiang, & Schweinhart, 2006). In another study investigating *block play* (building/constructing/learning with blocks), there was a strong correlation between block play experiences in preschool and standardized math scores in seventh grade and again in high school. The researchers suggested that construction play with blocks offers the preschool age child opportunities to classify, measure, count, order, use fractions, and explore depth, width, length, symmetry, shape and space—skills that provide the foundation for later, more formal cognitive instruction involved in learning mathematics, suggesting a positive correlation between preschool block play and later mathematical success (Wolfgang, Stannard, & Jones, 2001).

The following indicators have been identified as key attributes of cognitive development and general knowledge:

- Observation; questioning; problem solving
- Recognizing and understanding relationships, associations, differences, and similarities among people, objects, and events
- Comparing and contrasting
- Ability to construct, understand, acquire, and represent knowledge
- Physical knowledge
  - o Awareness of the physical world
    - Understanding the properties of objects, people, and events
    - Recognizing and identifying colors
- Logico-mathematical knowledge
  - o Understanding numeric concepts
    - Counting, recognizing, writing, and sequencing numbers
  - o Shapes
  - o Understanding concepts of time
    - Sequencing events
  - o Having the ability to sort, classify, and order objects
  - o Recognizing and identifying shapes and patterns
- Social-conventional knowledge
  - o Having knowledge of personal data (name, age, phone number)
  - o Distinguishing real from pretend
  - o Making connections and building on prior knowledge
  - o Relating cause to effect
  - o Making predictions
  - o Understanding conventions and the purpose of rules
  - o Understanding adult roles
  - o Complying with teacher and authority figures

Figure 2.1 Kindergarten Readiness: A New Model

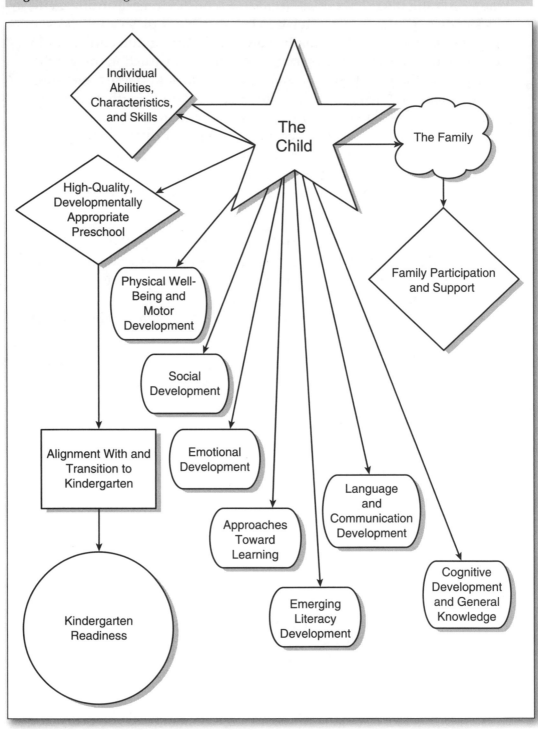

Source: Cappelloni, 2010.

CONCLUSION

It is widely recognized that experiences in all domains of early learning and development benefit young children and help them in their readiness for school. By addressing learning opportunities in all of the seven domains—the components of the multidimensional framework of kindergarten readiness—children will build important readiness abilities that will help prepare them for the transition to kindergarten.

PROFESSIONAL DEVELOPMENT DISCUSSION GUIDE

1. Deepen Your Thinking:

   a. Choose one or more of these individual inquiry topics for group discussion:

      i. What are the seven domains of early learning and development?

      ii. Choose one domain.

         1. What are the indicators for that domain?

         2. Why are the indicator's skills, abilities, and characteristics important for children to be able to do successfully?

         3. What are some examples that demonstrate proficiency in each domain?

WHERE CAN I LEARN MORE?

California Department of Education http://www.cde.ca.gov/index.asp

Child Trends http://www.childtrends.org/

Early Childhood Research and Practice (ECRP) http://ecrp.uiuc.edu/

Frank Porter Graham Child Development Institute http://fpg.unc.edu

International Reading Association http://www.reading.org

National Association for the Education of Young Children http://www.naeyc.org/

National Center for Education Statistics http://nces.ed.gov

National Institute for Early Education Research http://www.nieer.org

National Institutes of Health (NIH) http://www.nih.gov/

National Reading Panel (NRP) http://www.nationalreadingpanel.org/

United States Department of Education http://www.ed.gov/

3 What Do Young Children Need to Know and Be Able to Do to Be *Ready* for Kindergarten?

The current movement to improve student achievement through stronger accountability for schools is one of the most significant developments in education today. Schools are increasingly accountable for making sure that students perform to meet specific benchmarks. Grade level standards have been written to articulate what students are expected to learn, how they are expected to perform, and what teachers are expected to teach in Grades K–12.

Increased academic standards and assessments of all students' progress towards meeting those standards have placed growing pressure on teachers, students, and their families. Many early childhood professionals agree that kindergarten today has become academically oriented to the extent that it resembles first grade. It has been suggested that this movement toward greater accountability has significantly impacted early childhood education's attempts to provide greater accountability for learning outcomes during the preschool years (Scott-Little, Lesko, Martella, & Milburn, 2007).

It is generally agreed that (1) children entering kindergarten demonstrate greater proficiencies in some areas than others; (2) all children demonstrate varying degrees of school readiness; and (3) readiness comprises many indicators within the different domains of early learning and development. However, the degree of importance placed on proficiencies in each of the different domains varies considerably between stakeholders. Studies have indicated that policymakers, legislators, administrators, parents, preschool teachers, and kindergarten teachers vary widely in their expectations regarding what children should know and be able to do before beginning kindergarten (Hains, Fowler, Schwartz, Kottwitz, & Rosenkoetter, 1989; O'Donnell, 2008; Piotrkowski, Botsko, & Matthews, 2000; Wesley & Buysse, 2003).

EARLY LEARNING STANDARDS

Recent research indicating that children's experiences before they begin kindergarten are critically important for their future school success has helped fuel the momentum during the last decade in developing early learning standards in early childhood education. These early learning standards were developed to help define what a child should be expected to know and be able to do upon kindergarten entry and to establish criteria for what should be taught in publicly funded preschools to ensure children's success in kindergarten and beyond.

The National Association for the Education of Young Children (NAEYC) and the National Association of Early Childhood Specialists in

State Departments of Education (NAECS/SDE) assert, like the National Institute for Early Education Research (NIEER), that early learning standards are a valuable component of a comprehensive, high-quality early childhood education and that these standards help promote school readiness and later academic and social competence. The implementation of early learning standards, therefore, can help build consistency and continuity, support better transitions from preschool to kindergarten, and contribute to an approach closely aligned with K–12 standards and performance expectations (NAEYC & NAECS/SDE, 2002).

Early learning standards are documents that articulate what should be taught and what children should learn prior to kindergarten entry. Although all states require early childhood classrooms to meet *some* specific quality standards in order to receive state preschool funds, each state has its own criteria for individual early learning standards (Barnett, Epstein, Carolan, Fitzgerald, Ackerman, & Friedman, 2010).

Early learning standards were primarily developed for use in publicly funded preschool programs to improve teaching practices. There is a large disparity among the 50 states regarding the use of early learning standards. The development, content, implementation, and evaluation of early learning standards varies from state to state. In some states, they are voluntary, and in other states, they are mandatory. Some states monitor the use of early learning standards in preschools and provide training and technical assistance to teachers. Some states align their standards with curriculum and assessments, while in other states, the early learning standards are available, but there is no accountability for their implementation. Some states do not have assessments in place at all to measure children's progress articulated in the standards. Furthermore, only 13 states explicitly state that the purpose of their early learning standards is to improve children's readiness for school or to at least increase the likelihood that children will learn skills important for kindergarten entry (Scott-Little, Kagan, & Frelow, 2003a, 2003b, 2005).

A number of concerns have been raised regarding the appropriateness of any standards in early educational settings. These include (1) potential negative impacts and limitations for children with disabilities and children from homes whose primary language is not English; (2) the belief that the very nature of young children's development does not lend itself to standards; and (3) the belief that standards for preschool-age children are counter to what is known about children's growth and development and may shift instructional methods more toward teacher-directed rather than child-initiated approaches (Copple & Bredekamp, 2009; Scott-Little et al., 2003b, 2007).

Not only is there great variability in the use, purpose, and alignment of early learning standards with K–12 standards, but there is an overwhelmingly strong emphasis in the domains of language and communication development and cognitive development and general knowledge. The domains of social and emotional development and approaches toward learning are very underrepresented in the standards (Scott-Little, Kagan, & Frelow, 2006).

Scott-Little et al. (2005, 2006, 2007) postulated that this emphasis on the more academic domains may have been due to a number of factors: (1) some states viewed these skills as more important for readiness than the other domains; (2) there was a greater body of research literature in the areas of early literacy and cognition, enabling states to articulate standards in these areas more easily than in approaches toward learning and social and emotional development, which can be more ambiguous and more difficult to operationalize; and (3) these domains lent themselves to more direct instruction, observation, and assessment, and therefore are represented to a greater extent in the standards. In some states, early learning standards are viewed as an extension downward of the K–12 standards, with an emphasis placed on the consistency between the two sets of standards. Since K–12 standards are academic in nature, other domains in the early learning standards, such as in the areas of social and emotional development and approaches toward learning, may have been left out because there were no corresponding K–12 standards. Overall, the strong emphasis that states have placed on the academic, content-related domains and the weak emphasis on the social, emotional, and behavioral approaches toward learning reflect how states have conceptualized readiness and what states have claimed children need to know and be able to do prior to kindergarten (Scott-Little et al., 2005, 2006, 2007).

Whereas the states' emphasis in early learning standards is clearly focused on the cognitive and language domains, recent research in neuroscience supports the healthy development in *all* domains of early learning and development. Not only has it been found that social and emotional development are highly correlated with children's learning and school success but positive early childhood experiences in *all* domains are essential for promoting social competency and school readiness and are associated with and are often predictors of later academic success (Bowman, Donovan, & Burns, 2001; Boyd, Barnett, Bodrova, Leong, & Gomby, 2005; LaParo & Pianta, 2000; Shonkoff & Phillips, 2000; Strickland & Riley-Ayers, 2006).

HIGH-QUALITY PRESCHOOL EDUCATION

Recent research suggests that attendance in high-quality preschool programs is associated with children's academic achievement in kindergarten and has long-term effects on children's social and emotional outcomes

(Barnett & Yarosz, 2007; Boyd et al., 2005; Copple & Bredekamp, 2009; Zill, 1999) as well as on academic achievement later in school (Bowman et al., 2001; Shonkoff & Phillips, 2000; Snow, Burns, & Griffin, 1998; West, Denton, & Germino Hausken, 2000).

NAEYC and NAECS/SDE also assert that high-quality early childhood education can nurture physical, social, emotional, language, and intellectual development. There is evidence that children who have attended preschool programs, prekindergarten, or Head Start enter kindergarten with more proficiencies and have lower rates of kindergarten retention and special education placement than those children who have not attended such programs. Children who attended one or two years of a preschool program showed cognitive gains in math and literacy and more positive outcomes in classroom behavior, self-esteem, and motivation (Boyd et al., 2005; Lunenburg, 2000; Magnuson, Ruhm, & Waldfogel, 2007).

KINDERGARTEN TEACHERS' READINESS VIEWS

Research on teaching effectiveness suggests that the beliefs teachers hold about the curriculum, their students, and their roles and responsibilities directly influence their instructional practice and expectations in the classroom (Hair, Halle, Terry-Humen, Lavelle, & Calkins, 2006; Pajares, 1992; Piotrkowski et al., 2000; Scott-Little et al., 2006). Kindergarten teachers' readiness views and expectations have been shown to have a tremendous impact on the emphasis of their instructional strategies, their intervention and retention practices, and on their transitional practices for children entering kindergarten (Bowman et al., 2001; Lin, Lawrence, & Gorrell, 2003; Rimm-Kaufman, Pianta, & Cox, 2000; Snider & Roehl, 2007). Therefore, it is essential to understand kindergarten teachers' perceptions about what characteristics, behaviors, and skills are important for children's success when they begin school.

Two large-scale studies conducted by the National Center for Education Statistics (NCES) in 1993 and 1999 used nationally representative samples of kindergarten teachers for the purpose of collecting data on their background characteristics, instructional practices, and beliefs about kindergarten readiness. The first study (Heaviside & Farris, 1993) was conducted at the request of the National Education Goals Panel (NEGP) as a component in the process of developing consensus on the definition of school readiness. This 1993 NCES survey asked kindergarten teachers to rate the importance of 15 characteristics of readiness according to their personal beliefs. Response options were given on a 5-point scale ranging from "not at all important" to "essential." Additional information was gathered about the teachers' classroom practices and their background characteristics and demographics.

Ninety-six percent of the kindergarten teachers in this study reported that being physically healthy, rested, and well-nourished was either "very important" or "essential" for kindergarten readiness; 84 percent believed that the child's ability to communicate his or her needs, wants, and thoughts verbally in the child's primary language was "very important" or "essential"; and 76 percent of the teachers believed that enthusiasm and curiosity in approaching new activities was "very important" or "essential." Other characteristics that teachers rated as "very important" or "essential" were the ability to follow directions (60 percent), not being disruptive in class (60 percent), being sensitive to other children's feelings (58 percent), and the ability to take turns and share (56 percent). Teachers ranked as "not at all important" problem-solving skills (24 percent), the ability to identify colors and shapes (24 percent), the ability to use pencils and paintbrushes (21 percent), alphabet knowledge (10 percent), and the ability to count to 20 or more (7 percent). Responses also indicated that teachers were unanimous in their belief that parents have an important role in preparing children for school. Ninety-nine percent of teachers believed that parents should read to their children and play counting games at home regularly, yet only 27 percent of the teachers believed that parents should make sure that their children know the alphabet before they begin kindergarten. Teachers were almost unanimous (94 percent) in their belief that it is the teacher's responsibility to build readiness skills in the kindergarten classroom once the child begins school. Most teachers (88 percent) also felt that readiness is developmental and cannot be forced (Heaviside & Farris, 1993, p.8).

In the second large-scale NCES study, the Early Childhood Longitudinal Study (ECLS 1998–1999), the kindergarten class of 1998–1999 cohort followed a sample of children from kindergarten through the eighth grade. This study also found that kindergarten teachers perceived social attributes as more important than academic skills. Almost 84 percent of the teachers rated "tells needs/thoughts" as "very important" or "essential"; 79 percent rated "not disruptive of the class" as "very important" or "essential"; 78 percent rated "follows directions" as "very important" or "essential"; and 74 percent rated "take turns and shares" as "very important" or "essential." In comparison, less than 15 percent rated "counts to 20 or more" as "very important" or "essential"; 21 percent rated "knows most of the alphabet" as "very important" or "essential"; and 32 percent rated "names colors and shapes" as "very important" or "essential" (Lin et al., 2003).

NCES is currently in a new phase—the ECLS 2010–2011 study. The kindergarten class of 2010–11 cohort will follow a sample of children from kindergarten through the fifth grade. This study will continue to investigate and provide national data on children's transitions to nonparental care, early education programs, and school. The ECLS study will provide data to analyze relationships among a range of family, school, community, and individual variables regarding children's early learning, development, and school performance (NCES, 2012).

In these and in other related studies investigating kindergarten teachers' beliefs about school readiness, many kindergarten teachers expressed concerns and reported that a significant number of children do not enter kindergarten optimally ready to learn (Piotrkowski et al., 2000). They reported that a lack of preschool experience, a lack of family support for teaching necessary readiness skills, disruptiveness, and a child's inability to communicate needs and thoughts are factors that impact a child's readiness for kindergarten (Heaviside & Farris, 1993; Lin et al., 2003; Wesley & Buysse, 2003). In a national survey of 3,595 kindergarten teachers, 46 percent of the teachers reported that more than half of their students began kindergarten with a number of problems, one of which was that they were unable to follow directions (Rimm-Kaufman et al., 2000).

Overall, these studies investigating teachers' perceptions about kindergarten readiness suggest that kindergarten teachers placed the greatest importance on children's physical health; on social aspects of readiness (such as following directions and being sensitive to other children's feelings); on children's abilities to communicate needs, wants, and thoughts verbally; and on children's approaching new activities with enthusiasm and curiosity. Kindergarten teachers placed much less emphasis on the importance of academic skills (such as entering kindergarten knowing the letters of the alphabet or being able to count to 20 or above). Further, most teachers agreed that readiness for school occurs as children mature and grow and cannot be pushed, regardless of the pressure many kindergarten teachers have expressed feeling due to school standards, kindergarten exit skills and assessments, and first grade teachers (Wesley & Buysse, 2003). Overall, teachers have reported that it is their responsibility to teach the skills children will need in kindergarten *during* the kindergarten year and that pre-academic skills are not as important for entering kindergartners as other, nonacademic readiness skills. Kindergarten teachers, preschool teachers, and families concur that a child's overall health, compliance with teacher authority, social and emotional maturity, self-care, and eagerness to learn are all very important readiness skills (Piotrkowski et al., 2000).

PRESCHOOL TEACHERS' AND PARENTS' READINESS BELIEFS

To make things more problematic, however, kindergarten teachers' beliefs about readiness are often inconsistent with those of preschool teachers and parents (Hains, et al., 1989; Piotrkowski et al., 2000; Wesley & Buysse, 2003). Kindergarten and preschool teachers have been shown to agree that characteristics such as confidence, creativity, and curiosity are more important than academic skills, but preschool teachers have also expressed concern that children exiting preschool are unprepared for the academic demands of kindergarten (Hains, et al., 1989; Piotrkowski et al., 2000; Wesley & Buysse, 2003). Parents' readiness beliefs have also been closely aligned with those of kindergarten teachers, although, like preschool teachers, they have placed greater urgency on children's academic skills. Findings from the Parents' Reports of the School Readiness of Young Children from the National Household Education Surveys Program of 2007 (O'Donnell, 2008) indicated that 56 percent of parents of preschoolers reported that it was essential to teach their children the alphabet; 54 percent of parents felt that it was essential to teach their children numbers; and 45 percent of parents felt that it was essential to teach their children to read before entering kindergarten. Many parents have feared that their children are starting school unprepared for the tasks expected of them (Iruka & Carver 2006; Wesley & Buysse, 2003), but at the same time, parents have expressed concern in their own abilities to teach their children these academic abilities (Wesley & Buysse, 2003).

Most recently, in 2010, Cappelloni conducted a study to investigate kindergarten teachers' perceptions of kindergarten readiness. The foundation for Cappelloni's survey instrument was Scott-Little, Kagan, and Frelow's (2005) content analysis of states' early learning standards. These researchers used the National Education Goals Panel (NEGP) framework (Kagan, Moore, & Bredekamp, 1995) as the foundation for their system of coding and analyzing the states' early learning standards in their study. They found the NEGP framework to be the closest approximation to a national consensus on areas of early learning and development, and it provided them with a framework to code the content of the standards and operationalize indicators for each of the NEGP's five domains: physical well-being and motor development, social and emotional development, approaches toward learning, language development, and cognitive development and general knowledge. Key attributes within the standards were examined, and the researchers subsequently developed 36 indicators across the five domains that articulated specific skills and knowledge for each.

Cappelloni (2010) built on the Scott-Little et al. study (2005), expanding the five domains to seven: (1) physical well-being and motor development, (2) emotional development, (3) social development, (4) approaches toward learning, (5) language development and communication, (6) emerging literacy, and (7) cognitive development and general knowledge. Forty-three indicators across those domains were articulated to specify particular skills, abilities, knowledge, and characteristics for each domain in order to investigate the degree of importance kindergarten teachers placed on each of the domains and the specific indicators in each domain. Tests for internal reliability indicated that the domains (scales) can be measured reliably, and the survey instrument demonstrated both content and construct validity.

Reponses to the 43 items in the survey, *Kindergarten Teachers' Perceptions of Kindergarten Readiness,* collected from 653 kindergarten teachers, provided the data for the study. The data analysis revealed that, consistent with prior research (Hains et al., 1989; Heaviside & Farris, 1993; Lin et al., 2003; Piotrkowski et al., 2000; Rimm-Kaufman et al., 2000; Wesley & Buysse, 2003), kindergarten teachers indicated that overall they perceived the nonacademic abilities and characteristics of kindergarten readiness (such as social, emotional, and behavioral skills and abilities) as having the greatest importance (Cappelloni, 2010).

At the item level, kindergarten teachers in the Cappelloni study (2010) perceived that the most important characteristic for kindergarten readiness was having self-help skills. Following this item, teachers ranked items pertaining to emotional maturity, self-regulatory behavior, social relationships and interactions, enthusiasm toward learning, and sensitivity and respect toward others also as "very important" or "essential." They rated items pertaining to early literacy, numeracy, and other cognitive abilities pertaining to memory and reasoning as the least important. Teachers were unanimous in their belief (92.5 percent of the teachers rated this as "very important" or "essential") that *self-help skills* were the most important of all the kindergarten readiness indicators. Between 60 percent and 74 percent of the teachers also rated items regarding compliance with authority, ability to separate from parents, respecting others, cooperation, enthusiasm toward learning, self-control, sharing, and taking turns as "very important" or "essential." Teachers ranked abilities and skills pertaining to academic areas as much less important. These included items relating to math concepts, early literacy, phonemic awareness, memory, and logic.

Upon close inspection of the teachers' ratings of the 43 individual items in the Cappelloni study (2010; Table 3.1), it can be concluded that kindergarten teachers believed that characteristics from *all* the constructs are important to varying degrees, suggesting that kindergarten teachers believe that a well-balanced, developmentally appropriate approach to learning and development should strengthen a child's skills in *all* domains without focusing on narrowly defined skills. Kindergarten teachers might perceive academic skills to be more appropriately taught in kindergarten rather than social skills and emotional development, which they believe children should be taught and experience prior to kindergarten. Perhaps kindergarten teachers believe it is their responsibility to teach the skills children will need in kindergarten *during* the kindergarten year, with the provision that children are healthy and well-rested, are able to communicate their needs and wants effectively, and follow teachers' directions, take turns, and share.

Additionally, through the application of a factor analysis (a statistical method of grouping like items together), a new conceptualization of kindergarten readiness emerged. It was discovered that kindergarten teachers recognized the interrelatedness of all the domains. Items that had previously appeared conceptually different and unrelated were now shown to be associated with one another, suggesting new relationships among readiness characteristics, abilities, and skills that do not operate alone, but collectively (Cappelloni, 2010).

For example, a child's attentiveness, initiative, task persistence, and ease in making transitions are not only associated with but are in part dependent on the child's independence. The child's ability to communicate needs and use appropriate vocabulary are skills helpful in developing friendships, playing, and cooperating with other children. A child's self-control and independence are linked to the child's self-help skills; positive classroom behavior is linked to compliance with authority; and fine motor control is associated with learning colors and shapes.

Results of the Cappelloni study (2010) indicate that kindergarten teachers today hold similar beliefs about readiness as they have during the past twenty years, suggesting that the most important skills and abilities that prepare children for kindergarten encompass characteristics pertaining to their emotional maturity, self-regulation, eagerness to learn, compliance with authority, respect for others, communication and interactions with peers and adults, and overall good physical health. Teachers' views in the Cappelloni study were consistent with teachers' views in prior studies, which indicated that academic abilities were not important readiness skills, suggesting instead that these skills are more appropriately taught during, not prior to, kindergarten. This is particularly interesting when considering the current educational climate of increased accountability, more rigorous K–12 state content standards, and, more specifically, the demanding academic expectations in kindergarten.

Children's effective functioning in the kindergarten classroom and early academic success depend on strengths in all areas of learning and development prior to kindergarten. The fact that there has been little change over time in what kindergarten teachers believe to be important, despite current pressures for students to perform to higher grade-level standards, is impressive. This recognition of the importance of social and emotional development on early learning and later academic success conforms with research findings in early childhood development.

Table 3.1 Ranked Order of Survey Items (1–43) From Greatest to Least in "Kindergarten Teachers' Perceptions of Kindergarten Readiness"

Kindergarten Readiness Survey Items	Percentage of Teachers Choosing "Very Important" or "Essential"
Demonstrates self-help skills	92.5
Compliance with teacher and authority figures	73.6
Separates from parent without anxiety	71.5
Respects rights of others by keeping hands to self/keeps to own space	67.9
Cooperates and plays with other children	66.5
Shows enthusiasm, eagerness, and curiosity	64.5
Self-control and positive classroom behavior	64.2
Shares and takes turns	61.9
Appears to be in overall good physical health	60.9
Communicates needs/wants/thoughts in primary language	59.3
Shows sensitivity to other children's feelings	49.2
Follows two-step directions	48.2
Listens attentively to story for 10 or more minutes	47.6
Self-confidence in abilities and pride in work	45.6
Attentiveness to activity/task for 10+ minutes	45.0
Uses classroom materials appropriately	44.6
Expresses emotions and feelings effectively	43.5
Communicates and interacts with adults effectively	43.5
Forms new friendships with peers	43.3
Transitions from one activity to another without problems	39.4

(Continued)

(Continued)

Kindergarten Readiness Survey Items	Percentage of Teachers Choosing "Very Important" or "Essential"
Demonstrates independence: completes activity/task on own	39.2
Understands word meaning/uses age-appropriate vocabulary	35.8
Task persistence: follows through on difficult tasks	34.2
Shows initiative: begins tasks on own	33.9
Can write own name	31.2
Observes, asks questions, solves problems	30.5
Identifies colors and basic geometric shapes	29.4
Communicates needs/wants/thoughts in English	28.5
Good fine motor skills: uses scissors, Legos, glue stick	28.3
Resolves conflict by using compromise strategies	27.6
Good graphomotor skills: correct pencil grip, traces	25.9
Good gross motor skills: jumps, hops, skips, runs	23.3
Recognizes and knows most letter names	21.6
Recognizes and states similarities and differences between two objects	16.5
Retells familiar story and sequences events	10.7
Can write most letters of the alphabet	10.4
Recognizes and writes numbers to 10 or above	10.1
Produces rhyming words	8.5
Counts to 20 or above	7.7
Identifies most letter sounds	6.7
Can state story structure after listening to a story	4.3
Can read five or more sight words	3.7
Understands concepts of time/associates activities with time of day	3.1

N = 653 teacher participant within this study.

Source: Cappelloni, 2010.

COMMON CORE CONTENT STANDARDS

Another way to consider which readiness skills might be helpful during the preschool years is to look ahead and examine the skills and abilities that children are expected to know and be able to do at the *end* of kindergarten. Knowing this information can be helpful in determining what will be helpful as preparation for this undertaking. Public kindergartens are accountable for teaching content aligned with their individual state's kindergarten State Content Standards and kindergarten Common Core State Standards (CCSS). The mission statement of the Common Core State Standards Initiative (2011) states,

> The Common Core State Standards provide a consistent, clear understanding of what students are expected to learn, so teachers and parents know what they need to do to help them. The standards are designed to be robust and relevant to the real world, reflecting the knowledge and skills that our young people need for success in college and careers. . . . The standards are informed by the highest, most effective models from states across the country and countries around the world, and provide teachers and parents with a common understanding of what students are expected to learn. Consistent standards will provide appropriate benchmarks for all students, regardless of where they live.

The CCSS are currently adopted by 45 states and 3 territories. They are only currently available in the content areas of English Language Arts and Mathematics. A summary of the topics they include are listed in Resource 3.1. For complete kindergarten CCCS, see Resources 4.4 and 4.5.

Resource 3.1 Summary of Kindergarten Common Core Content Standards

Kindergarten: English Language Arts

1. Reading: Literature
   Key Ideas and Details
   Craft and Structure
   Integration of Knowledge and Ideas
   Range of Reading and Level of Text Complexity

(Continued)

(Continued)

2. Reading: Informational Text

Key Ideas and Details
Craft and Structure
Integration of Knowledge and Ideas
Range of Reading and Level of Text Complexity

3. Reading: Foundational Skills

Print Concepts
Phonological Awareness
Phonics and Word Recognition
Fluency

4. Writing

Text Types and Purposes
Production and Distribution of Writing
Research to Build and Present Knowledge

5. Speaking and Listening

Comprehension and Collaboration
Presentation of Knowledge and Ideas

6. Language

Conventions of Standard English
Vocabulary Acquisition and Use

Kindergarten: Mathematics

1. Counting and Cardinality

Know number names and the count sequence.
Count to tell the number of objects.
Compare numbers.

2. Operations and Algebraic Thinking

Understand addition as putting together and adding to, and understand subtraction as taking apart and taking from.

3. Number and Operations in Base Ten

Work with numbers 11–19 to gain foundations for place value.

4. Measurement and Data

Describe and compare measurable attributes.
Classify objects and count the number of objects in each category.

5. Geometry

Identify and describe shapes (squares, circles, triangles, rectangles, hexagons, cubes, cones, cylinders, and spheres).
Analyze, compare, create, and compose shapes.

For more detailed information on the specifics of these standards, visit the Common Core State Standards website: http://www.corestandards.org/

CONCLUSION

It is interesting to note that despite the increased accountability and the push for higher academic benchmarks and rigorous expectations in kindergarten, kindergarten teachers' beliefs regarding what is important for children to know and be able to do prior to kindergarten have changed little over time. Overall, kindergarten teachers place the most emphasis on children's social abilities—particularly sharing, taking turns, and being sensitive to the needs of others. Kindergarten teachers also rated enthusiasm and curiosity, following directions, compliance with authority, communicating needs and wants effectively, self-help skills, and self-control as important skills for kindergarten.

Additionally, kindergarten teachers have recently recognized important relationships, associations, and interactions between the domains of early learning and development that bring relevance to creating developmentally appropriate curriculum that strengthens children's readiness skills. Chapter 4 will discuss creating an early childhood educational curriculum specifically aimed at addressing readiness for kindergarten.

PROFESSIONAL DEVELOPMENT DISCUSSION GUIDE

1. Deepen Your Thinking:

    a. Choose one or more of these individual inquiry topics for group discussion:

        i. Only 10 percent or less of all teachers in the Cappelloni study rated items from both the domains of cognitive development and emerging literacy, as "very important" or "essential." The single item, "Child can read five or more sight words," was rated by 88 percent of the teachers as "not too important" or "somewhat important," suggesting that academic skills should be taught once children *enter* kindergarten rather than as preparation *for* kindergarten.

            1. How do you and your professional learning community feel about teaching specific academic skills, such as reading words, in your preschool?

            2. What do you believe families want you to focus on?

            3. Are your beliefs consistent with those of the families?

WHERE CAN I LEARN MORE?

Common Core State Standards Initiative http://www.corestandards.org/

National Association for the Education of Young Children (NAEYC) http://naeyc.org

National Association of Early Childhood Specialists in State Departments of Education (NAECS/SDE) http://www.naecs-sde.org

National Center for Educational Research http://ies.ed.gov/ncer/

National Institute for Early Education Research (NIEER) http://nieer.org

4 The Developmentally Appropriate Curriculum

THE NEED FOR A DEVELOPMENTALLY APPROPRIATE CURRICULUM

The acquisition of a child's readiness skills can be traced back to family characteristics and influences during the years before kindergarten, including the child's preschool experiences (Shonkoff & Phillips, 2000; West, Denton, & Germino Hausken, 2000; Zill & West, 2001). The growing evidence that early childhood experiences are intricately linked to later school success has fueled recent interest in the importance of making sure that all children entering kindergarten are ready to learn. Recent research indicates that a high-quality preschool experience is associated with academic achievement in kindergarten and has long-term social and emotional outcomes. Early education approaches that encourage social interactions, language experiences, and social-emotional development can tremendously impact a young child's development (Thompson, 2008).

Preschool has been shown to benefit *all* children and prepare them for the transition to the accelerated academic demands of kindergarten (Barnett, Epstein, Friedman, Boyd, & Hustedt, 2008; Barnett & Yarosz, 2007; Head Start Bureau, 2005; Magnuson, Ruhm, & Waldfogel, 2007; Marcon, 2002). More specifically, children considered to be at risk of school failure benefit particularly from a high-quality preschool (Logue, 2007; West et al., 2000).

Current research supports the claim that the years before kindergarten are recognized by a vitally important period of early brain development and learning (Bowman, Donovan, & Burns, 2001; Shannon, 2007; Shonkoff & Phillips, 2000; Thompson, 2008). The first five years in a child's life are a time of extraordinary physical, social, emotional, linguistic, and conceptual development. Recent advances in developmental neuroscience provide greater insight into early brain development, revealing that brain development is an ongoing, complex interplay between the child's active mind and the child's environment (Copple & Bredekamp, 2009; Kagan, Moore, & Bredekamp, 1995; Shonkoff & Phillips, 2000; Thompson, 2008). Learning during these early years occurs in all areas of a young child's development—physical/motor, social, emotional, approaches toward learning, language and communication, emerging literacy, and cognitive development and general knowledge. Developmentally appropriate experiences that stimulate the brain's activity through engagement and stimulation help children become more proficient at cognitive functions, attention, behavior, and emotions. Social and emotional development is highly correlated with children's learning and school success. Positive early childhood experiences in all domains are essential for promoting social competency and school readiness and are associated with (and are often predictors of) later academic success (Bowman et al., 2001; Boyd, Barnett, Bodrova, Leong, & Gomby, 2005; LaParo & Pianta, 2000; Shonkoff & Phillips, 2000; Strickland & Riley-Ayers, 2006).

It has recently been recognized that the domains of early learning and development are interrelated and interconnected, suggesting that they do not operate in isolation from one another. The development of these domains, however, is largely dependent on the early childhood educational settings to which children have access—specifically, the availability of high-quality, developmentally appropriate preschools. The National Association for the Education of Young Children (NAEYC) and the National Association of Early Childhood Specialists in State Departments of Education (NAECS/SDE) have asserted that high-quality early childhood education can nurture the physical, social, emotional, language, and intellectual development in young children (NAEYC & NAECS/SDE, 2002). Research suggests that attendance at high-quality preschool programs is associated with children's academic achievement in kindergarten and has long-term effects on children's social and emotional outcomes (Barnett & Yarosz, 2007; Boyd et al., 2005; Copple & Bredekamp, 2009; Zill, 1999) and on academic achievement later in school (Bowman et al., 2001; Shonkoff & Phillips, 2000; Snow, Burns, & Griffin, 1998; West et al., 2000).

Therefore, the purpose of this chapter is to encourage the development of skills and abilities across all the domains of early learning and development. This chapter is intended as a resource to help teachers plan a balanced, integrated, and developmentally appropriate learning experience to strengthen important kindergarten readiness skills, abilities, and characteristics.

There is evidence that children who have attended preschool, prekindergarten, or Head Start programs enter kindergarten with more proficiencies and have lower rates of kindergarten retention and special education placement than those children who have not attended such programs. Children who attend one or two years of a preschool program show cognitive gains in math and literacy and more positive outcomes in classroom behavior, self-esteem, and motivation (Boyd et al., 2005; Lunenburg, 2000; Magnuson et al., 2007). During the preschool years, important social and emotional development occurs in school, such as developing and sustaining social relationships with teachers and peers and developing emotional and social competence, all of which build a foundation for kindergarten readiness and later academic success. Research suggests that children who begin kindergarten with certain resources and positive social and emotional experiences are at a developmental advantage. The advantages as well as the disadvantages with which children begin school are also sustainable over time (Boyd et al., 2005; Shonkoff & Phillips, 2000).

DEVELOPMENTALLY APPROPRIATE PRACTICE

The core of developmentally appropriate practice (DAP), according to the NAEYC, is *intentionality*—purposeful and thoughtful teaching, identifying learning goals and desired outcomes, teaching toward those goals, building on what children already know, and aiming for goals that are challenging and achievable (NAEYC, 2009). NAEYC claims that in order to consider making developmentally appropriate decisions in working with young children, the educator must have knowledge of three things:

1. the stages and characteristics of child development, which informs what experiences will most likely promote children's learning and development,

2. each child's individual characteristics and how best to be responsive to meet the needs of each individual child,

3. the social and cultural contexts in which children live, including the values, expectations, and behavioral and linguistic conventions of each child's home environment, in order to ensure that learning experiences in school are meaningful, relevant, and respectful of each child and family (NAEYC, 2009).

NAEYC also identifies 12 interconnecting principles, founded in research and theory, that drive DAP. To summarize, these principles recognize that

- all domains of early learning and development are important, interrelated, and influenced by one another.
- rates of development and learning vary among children as well as within each child.
- building on previously acquired knowledge fosters the acquisition of new knowledge, skills, and learning.
- positive interactions with responsive adults and positive relationships with peers contribute to children's healthy development.
- children learn in a variety of different ways: A wide range of teaching strategies, learning experiences, materials, and opportunities for play support learning and development (NAEYC, 2009).

Now, how do we take these principals of DAP and embed them into research-based instructional practices to strengthen young children's learning and development in all domains?

Learning is a combination of social interactions and individual effort. Jean Piaget (1896–1980) claimed that children construct knowledge based on their experiences, through which the world is understood, interpreted, organized, and stored. Piaget theorized that learning is a process of making connections between new information and what is already known (Singer & Revenson, 1996). Piaget suggested that this preoperational stage of development could be labeled the "age of curiosity," since preschool age children constantly question and investigate new things (Darling-Hammond et al., 2009, p. 21). Lev Vygotsky (1896–1934) theorized that children learn through interactions with their environment and interactions with others. He claimed that all learning involves social interactions, in a social and cultural context (Vygotsky, 1978).

These learning theorists laid the foundation for *developmentally appropriate teaching* (Darling-Hammond et al., 2009), *developmentally appropriate practice,* and *intentional teaching* (NAEYC, 2009). These practices employ research-based instructional methods that are responsive to all domains of children's developmental readiness, that select developmentally appropriate tasks, and that tap into students' interests. Developmentally appropriate teaching encourages a wide variety of learning experiences, strategies, and materials to accommodate individual differences in learning and recognizes children's cultures and prior experiences while moving toward desired competencies.

Cognitive scientists have demonstrated that learning involves this process of making connections between what is already known and new information. For learning to occur, new ideas are related to old ones—children make connections based on what they already know, accessing prior knowledge and bridging it to new material (Darling-Hammond et al., 2009). Teachers help children build on prior learning by helping them make connections to and associations with objects, events, and things they already know. Teachers assist children in developing higher levels of competencies and complexity. Learning is strongly influenced by both adult-child social interactions and peer interactions that encourage students to learn from each other to optimize their learning.

Children in preschool have a wide variety of learning styles and needs and demonstrate a vast range of abilities and skills. Understanding differences in the way young children learn can help us guide their learning. By understanding the theories of multiple intelligences, differentiated instruction, the zone of proximal development, and scaffolding, teachers can help optimize learning opportunities for all children.

Children have different interests, abilities, and strengths that often serve as pathways to learning, providing them with different ways to understand and learn. Howard Gardner, in 1983, proposed an alternative theory of intelligence. He claimed that there are seven *intelligences:* linguistic, logical, bodily-kinesthetic, musical, spatial, interpersonal, and intrapersonal. He later added an eighth, naturalistic. Gardner proposed that children at a young age show *proclivities*, or *inclinations*, to specific intelligences (Armstrong, 1994). Most children have strengths in several areas. Incorporating these intelligences into instruction ensures that all students' learning strengths will be addressed and that children can demonstrate their abilities in numerous ways. By tapping into different intelligences, teachers can create powerful curricular activities that reach all children, finding various means and modalities to introduce and approach new topics and concepts through different points of entry (Darling-Hammond et al., 2009).

Differentiated instruction is the process of providing instruction to each child to meet his or her specific needs. You start with what each child knows and can do and then build the learning from there. Differentiated instruction is what Daggett refers to as "responsive" teaching rather than "one-size-fits-all" teaching (2008, p. 3). Differentiating instruction means meeting the child at his or her specific ability level and providing instruction from there. It means being responsive to the individual abilities of each child.

Differentiating instruction requires the knowledge of what Vygotsky called the *zone of proximal development (ZPD)*—the distance between what a learner can do on his or her own and what he or she can accomplish with assistance (Vygotsky, 1978). ZPD is based on the concept that a child learns best when given a task just beyond what he or she can do independently and is given assistance from a more skilled person, such as a teacher or a peer. The child progresses from what he or she can do independently to what he or she can do with assistance to what he or she will be able to perform independently, thus preparing him or her for even more demanding or complex tasks.

Scaffolding adjusts the level of support provided to assist the child in learning. Scaffolding is the process by which the teacher organizes teaching so that it meets the child's developmental stage, goals, interests, and abilities. The teacher breaks down tasks into small, sequential steps to simplify learning, bridging what the child already knows or can do independently to what the child can do with the support.

In order to achieve both the acquisition of *domain knowledge*—concepts, facts, and procedures—and *strategic knowledge*—the ability to make use of those concepts, facts, and procedures to solve problems and accomplish tasks (Collins, Brown, & Holum, 1991)—teachers will embrace teaching methods in which they model or demonstrate, provide frequent coaching and feedback, scaffold learning tasks according to the needs of each individual child, and provide opportunities for children to practice skills. Learning activities will be sequenced from simple to more complex, and cooperation and collaboration will be fostered and promoted to help students develop competencies in a wide range of domains (Collins et al., 1991; Darling-Hammond et al., 2009).

Various teaching strategies and evidence-based best practices that support developmentally appropriate teacher-directed instruction in which there are specific learning goals and desired outcomes include the use of

- connecting learning to the child's prior knowledge and experiences.
- demonstrating the task.
- modeling the task.
- explaining the task.
- scaffolding—providing support through specific steps needed for the child to progress.
- coaching—providing guidance and further support while the child attempts the task independently
- differentiating instruction so that individual needs and different learning styles are addressed.
- providing feedback to students.
- providing opportunities for practice.

Besides learning through teacher-directed instruction, children construct new knowledge through discovery, exploration, invention, investigation, experimentation, questioning, and inquiry—a constructivist model of learning. Children thrive on being actively involved in new learning experiences through hands-on active learning experiences with exposure to new materials and ideas, both inside and outside the classroom. Learning experiences that are meaningful, relevant, and authentic (real) help children learn best, as they connect new knowledge to existing knowledge and are challenged through an interactive and collaborative classroom environment.

Learning what children are expected to know and be able to do as they *exit* kindergarten provides preschool teachers with vital information to help them prepare young children to start kindergarten. By looking ahead not only to the *start* of kindergarten to learn what entering kindergartens will be learning and studying but to the *end* of kindergarten to learn what children are expected to master at the end of the kindergarten year, preschool teachers can optimally prepare preschool children in all domains of early learning and development to enter kindergarten prepared and ready to learn. This process begins by examining the Kindergarten Content Standards, which clearly articulate the core conceptual understandings and procedures that all students are expected to master. Since kindergarten state standards vary from state to state, only the Kindergarten Common Core Standards in Mathematics and English Language Arts, common to 45 states and 3 territories, are included as Resource 4.5 at the end of this chapter. *Remember, we are **not** encouraging the teaching of these standards, but we **do** encourage exposure to and familiarity with materials and activities in preparation for the acquisition of these skills in kindergarten.*

In order to strengthen children's abilities and skills in all domains, preschools should provide learning experiences in each domain, laying the foundation for subsequent development and learning in kindergarten. Exposure, practice, and exploration are key. Children learn at different rates and in different ways, and all children demonstrate strengths in some areas more than in others. Mastery of specific skills is *not* the focus or the goal. Areas for preschool children to explore and strengthen skills and abilities include encouragement in the following areas:

Physical Well-Being and Motor Development

Gross Motor Skills:

Jump, hop, skip, gallop, slide, walk backwards, climb, kick, run, tiptoe, jumping jacks, throw, catch, balance on one foot

Fine Motor Skills:

Use of crayons, scissors, paintbrush, glue stick, glue brushes, small Legos and blocks, and other small manipulative objects to squeeze, pinch, grasp, cut, rip, roll, and control

Sensorimotor Skills:

Finger painting, water play, sand table, parachute play, play with clay, rip paper

Graphomotor Skills:

Proper pencil grip; color and draw; trace and copy shapes, numbers, and letters; write one's own name, draw a person with head and body parts

Self-Help Skills:

Feed self; take care of bathroom needs; clean up after self

Social Development

Share and take turns, cooperate with other children, keep hands and body to self, form new friendships, encourage sensitivity toward others' feelings and positive relationships with teachers, resolve conflict nonaggressively

Emotional Development

Express emotions and feelings, self-regulate behavior, impulse control, self-confidence

Approaches toward Learning

Independence (completing a task on one's own), attentiveness to tasks and task persistence (following through on difficult tasks), smooth transitions between activities, adjustment to changes in routines, curiosity, accept new challenges and try new things, problem solve, enthusiasm and curiosity about learning

Emerging Literacy Development

Look at books independently, listen to stories, discuss books, verbal and written response to text, letter and sound correspondence, learn new vocabulary and word meaning, knowledge of environmental print (alphabet, labeling objects with words, student names), scribble (pre-writing), write letters and first name, distinguish fiction from nonfiction

Language and Communication Development

Attentive listening, ask and answer questions, engage in conversations with adults and peers, listen to others when they are speaking, sing, rhyme, communicate needs, wants, and thoughts clearly in English, follow two-step directions, retell familiar stories

Cognitive Development and General Knowledge

Identify colors and basic two-dimensional shapes; sort objects by attributes; recognize similarities, differences, and relationships among objects; sequence events in the order they occurred; understand concepts of time; count objects; recognize numbers; extend patterns; follow classroom rules; comply with teachers and authority

A MODEL OF DEVELOPMENTALLY APPROPRIATE LEARNING EXPERIENCES THAT INTEGRATE ALL DOMAINS OF EARLY LEARNING AND DEVELOPMENT

Exposing children to new skills and providing opportunities for children to practice those skills can be done in fun and authentic ways, ways in which development in all the domains is not isolated but integrated. Four examples of learning experiences that incorporate all domains are discussed below. Two of the experiences begin by introducing a book (Resources 4.1 and 4.2), one involves setting up a creative play center (Resource 4.3), and one involves scientific investigation (Resource 4.4).

AN INTEGRATED MODEL BEGINNING WITH LITERATURE

Books provide rich resources for integrating learning in all domains. Concept books and other nonfiction books provide children with information about the world around them. Books can encourage the understanding of different perspectives and a respect for cultural diversity. Books can increase children's vocabulary and stimulate their curiosity and imagination. Books can deepen cognitive processing by stimulating questioning, problem solving, and comparing and contrasting and by encouraging higher-level thinking skills. Children learn that books are meaningful and relevant. Best of all, good literature stimulates children's desire to read and helps them develop a lifelong love of reading.

Resource 4.1 Early Literacy and Social Development: The Link Between Children's Literature and Teaching Conflict Resolution

Over the past two decades, conflict and violent behavior have greatly increased in our nation's schools. Conflict evolves into violent behavior when children have neither the oral language skills nor the ability to cope with a given situation in an alternative way. Unfortunately, children today are living in an increasingly violent world and are exposed to aggression and violence at a very early age through television, toys, video games, and societal issues. Children's literature can be used as a meaningful and powerful tool to teach conflict resolution in the preschool classroom.

Contextualization through Literature

Children's literature provides a rich background in which problem-solving and conflict-resolution skills can be taught. Studies suggest that literature-based instruction can enhance children's development of empathy and positive values (Appl & Pratt, 2007; Pace & Podesta, 1999). A primary tenet of social cognitive theory states that children's understanding and interpretation of situations directly influence their subsequent behavior (Lemerise & Arsenio, 2000). Through thoughtfully selected children's literature, teachers can address many issues related to conflict resolution in a nonthreatening, developmentally appropriate manner. The use of literature can make conflict concrete and specific, not an abstraction. "Literature gives young children a window on the world outside themselves" (Feeney & Moravcik, 2005, p. 27). Through the use of literature, teachers can address problems safely in a classroom environment that supports and nurtures conflict resolution and positive social behavior.

Defining the Conflict

The use of children's literature can help children develop a deeper understanding of conflict. Characters in stories provide problem-solving solutions in specific settings (Palmer, 2001). Teachers can emphasize how characters model conflict-resolution strategies. Because these strategies are embedded in literature written specifically for children, they are understandable and realistic.

Literature can help children identify certain behaviors. Through story, examples of conflicts escalating and being resolved are brought to life. Feelings attached to conflicts can be illustrated. Children can learn how small conflicts often escalate into bigger ones. They can also learn how conflict can be prevented. Through their actions, characters illustrate different approaches and strategies for handling and resolving conflict (Collins, 2002). Conflict-resolution options available to a child become increased with greater knowledge and understanding. Children's vocabulary for discussing conflict resolution can also increase.

The use of literature can help children understand the cause and effect of a specific conflict. It can demonstrate explicitly that actions have consequences. Children can learn how certain behaviors contribute to a problem. They can learn how to make constructive use of conflict to move forward and can realize that there are different options for solving conflict. Through literature, children can learn how to solve problems and how to use conflict resolution methods in real-life situations. Stories can help children discover how to resolve conflict in ways that are not hurtful, destructive, or violent to others.

Themes in Conflict Resolution

Major themes found in children's literature selected for the purpose of teaching conflict resolution in the preschool classroom include the following:

- Conflict and Feelings
  - anger management
  - impulse control
- Conflict-Solving Ideas
  - expressing feelings
  - talking and listening
  - sharing and taking turns
  - compromising
  - working together
  - strategies for calming down
- Understanding Other Perspectives
  - kindness
  - empathy
  - trust
- Cooperation
  - caring
  - respect
  - helpfulness

(Continued)

(Continued)

Instructional Strategies

To build understanding before discussing the topic of conflict resolution, the teacher might ask students the following questions:

- What *is* a conflict?
- What kinds of conflicts have you been in?
- What kinds of conflicts have you seen or heard other people get in?
- What kinds of things do children get in conflicts about?

Having this discussion before reading the story can add meaning for children by giving conflict a context in which to understand the story. By discussing the story after reading it, the teacher can help children further understand the conflict and identify the following:

- What was the problem or conflict in the story about?
- Who was involved in the conflict?
- What did the characters do who created a conflict?
- What did the characters do to try to resolve the conflict?
- How did the conflict turn out?
- Why do you think there was a conflict?
- How could this conflict have been prevented?
- How would you feel if you were one of the characters in the story?
- How would you have done or tried to resolve the conflict?

Extension activities derived from the literature can help reinforce new concepts and also help children internalize problem situations. The teacher can help children identify conflict-resolution strategies, role-play by modeling those strategies, practice those strategies in class, and evaluate how those strategies worked. By understanding, modeling, practicing, and evaluating, children can become more proficient in resolving conflict in positive ways in real-life situations. "Literature and stories enable students to move back and forth between text and real life" (Collins, 2002, p. 17).

An Example of a Suggested Book for Teaching Conflict Resolution in the Preschool Classroom: *Matthew and Tilly* by Rebecca C. Jones Theme Addressed: Escalation of Conflict in a Friendship

Summary: Matthew and Tilly are best friends. They spend their days together selling lemonade, playing games, and enjoying each other's company. One day, however, Matthew and Tilly have an argument over a broken crayon. The argument escalates into name-calling, and finally, they decide to separate. While playing alone, each child initially relishes having things his own way but soon realizes that experiences are more fun when shared with a friend. Apologies are made, and soon, the two friends are playing together again.

Classroom Application: This book lends itself to a conversation about the use of language and derogatory or hurtful words. During a conflict, people often use highly charged, emotive language, which they often regret later. After reading the story, the teacher could guide children in defining the initial conflict and ask them to recall and discuss the language Matthew and Tilly used. The children could then practice alternative vocabulary that could be used in similar situations. Practice in the use of "I" statements could be embedded into the lesson.

Suggested Literature for Teaching Conflict Resolution in the Primary Classroom

Conflict and Feelings

Alexander and the Terrible, Horrible, No Good, Very Bad Day by Judith Viorst

Grandpa's Face by Eloise Greenfield

Hooway for Wodney Wat by Helen Lester

I'm Gonna Like Me by Jamie Lee Curtis and Laura Cornell

Me First by Helen Lester

Mean Soup by Betsy Everitt

Spinky Sulks by William Steig

The Grouchy Ladybug by Eric Carle

The Hating Book by Charlotte Zolotow

The Little Brute Family by Russell Hoban

The Teacher From the Black Lagoon by Mike Thaler

When I Feel Angry by Cornelia Maude Spelman

When Sophie Gets Angry—Really, Really Angry by Molly Bang

Anger Management and Impulse Control

It's Mine! by Leo Lionni

Loudmouth George and the Sixth-Grade Bully by Nancy Carlson

Matthew and Tilly by Rebecca C. Jones

Stop Picking on Me by Pat Thomas

The Owl and the Woodpecker by Brian Wildsmith

The Pig War by Betty Baker

The Quarreling Book by Charlotte Zolotow

Conflict-Solving Ideas: Expressing Feelings, Talking and Listening, Sharing and Taking Turns, Compromising, Working Together, and Strategies for Calming Down

Angel Child, Dragon Child by Michelle Maria Surat

Babar and the Wully-Wully by Lauren De Brunhoff

Bootsie Barker Bites by Barbara Bottner

Clancy's Coat by Eve Bunting

First Pink Light by Eloise Greenfield

(Continued)

(Continued)

It's Mine by Leo Lionni

Six Crows by Leo Lionni

The Butter Battle Book by Dr. Seuss

The Island of the Skog by Steven Kellogg

The Knight and the Dragon by Tomie dePaola

The Owl and The Woodpecker by Brian Wildsmith

The Pig War by Betty Baker

The Quarreling Book by Charlotte Zolotow

The Terrible Thing That Happened at Our House by Marge Blaine

The Zax by Dr. Seuss

Who's in Rabbit's House? By Verna Aardema

Understanding Other Perspectives: Kindness, Empathy, and Trust

Here Comes the Cat! by Frank Asch

Rainbow Fish and the Big Blue Whale by Marcus Pfister

Tar Beach by Faith Ringgold

The Chinese Mirror by Mirra Ginsburg

The Hating Book by Charlotte Zolotow

The True Story of the Three Little Pigs by Jon Scieszka

Two Bad Ants by Chris Van Allsburg

Cooperation: Caring, Respect, and Helpfulness

A Chair For My Mother by Vera B. Williams

Listen Buddy by Helen Lester

Mufaro's Beautiful Daughters by John Steptoe

Peter's Chair by Ezra Jack Keats

She Come Bringing Me That Little Baby Girl by Eloise Greenfield

Teammates by Peter Golenbock

The Big Pile of Dirt by Eleanor Clymer

Two Good Friends by Judy Delton

Ty's One-Man Band by Mildred Pitts Walter

Source: From *Teaching Conflict Resolution in the Primary School Classroom Through Children's Literature* (Doctoral paper), by N. Cappelloni and M. Niesyn, 2007, San Francisco, CA: University of San Francisco, School of Education. Reprinted with permission.

Resource 4.2 Preschool Lesson Plan Using Kindergarten English Language Arts Common Core Reading Standard

Key Ideas and Details:

1. With prompting and support, ask and answer questions about key details in a text.

2. With prompting and support, retell familiar stories, including key details.

3. With prompting and support, identify characters, settings, and major events in a story.

The goal of this standard, the *Key Ideas and Details,* is for students to be able to retell a familiar story, including the main characters, the setting, and the major events of the story, recalling important details that are key to the text. There are a number of activities the preschool teacher can implement, working both with a whole group and in small groups, that will scaffold children's ability to successfully retell a story with key elements and events, demonstrating their initial understanding of this concept. For the purpose of this sample lesson, we will use a story familiar to many children, *The Little Red Hen.*

In the tale *The Little Red Hen,* a hen finds a grain of wheat and asks for help from the other farmyard animals (a pig, a duck, and a cat) to plant it. However, no animal will volunteer to help her. At each subsequent stage (harvest, threshing, milling the wheat into flour, and baking the flour into bread), the hen again asks for help from the other animals, but again, she gets no assistance. Finally, the hen has finished—the bread has been baked, and she asks the animals who will help her *eat* the bread. This time, all the animals enthusiastically volunteer. However, she declines their help, stating that no one aided her in the preparation work, and so she eats it with her chicks, leaving none for anyone else. The moral of this story is that those who show no willingness to contribute to an end product do not deserve to enjoy the end product.

1. Whole-group activity: introduction to the story

    a. Building background knowledge and investigating prior knowledge
        i. Teacher asks the students these questions:

            1. Who has ever made bread? Who knows what bread is made from? How does the wheat turn into flour? How is bread made? (Explain to students about flour and the process of making bread.)

            2. Who knows anything about hens, cats, dogs, and pigs? What is the same about all of these animals? What is different? Where do they live? Do they talk and work around a barn?

        ii. Teacher tells students this is a folktale (explain *folktale*) and that this story is fiction (explain *fiction*) about a hen who lives with a cat, a dog, and a pig and that in this story, a hen works very hard to bake some bread. For English language learners, bring in some raw wheat, some flour, and some bread to help build the new vocabulary. Stop during

(Continued)

(Continued)

the reading to explain and demonstrate any unfamiliar words (i.e., *thresh*).

   iii. Teacher reads the story out loud to the class.

   iv. Teacher discusses the story and asks the students questions to check for understanding and help them make personal connections to the story:

     1. Who are the characters in this story?

     2. Where does the story take place (the setting)?

     3. Is this story fiction or nonfiction?

     4. What happened in the story first? Then what happened? What happened at the end?

     5. Why do you think the pig, the cat, and the dog didn't want to help the hen?

     6. How would you feel if you were the hen?

     7. Why do you think the hen told them that they couldn't have any of the bread?

     8. How would you feel if you were the pig, the cat, and the dog and the hen told you that you couldn't have any of the bread? What do you think those animals might do differently next time the hen asked for help?

     9. What would you have done if you were the hen? What would you have done if you were the pig, the dog, or the cat?

    10. What would you do if someone asked you for help? How would you feel if you asked someone for some help and they told you no?

    11. What was your favorite part of this story?

    12. What did this story remind you of?

  2. Whole-group class project:

    a. With teacher support, the class creates a storyboard mural of the story of *The Little Red Hen*. The children create the characters, a background of the setting (the barn), and they illustrate the different steps the hen took to make the bread, all in sequential order. Once the mural is done and it is hanging in the classroom, the students are encouraged to look at the pictures and retell the story to each other.

  3. Small-group reading

    a. Students in their small groups read individual copies of the book together in a guided reading group with a teacher. The teacher asks many of the same questions as above with the students to check for understanding, sequencing, and retelling.

      i. Students draw a picture of their favorite part of the story. They dictate to the teacher what they want to say, and the teacher writes it down at the bottom of their picture. These "response to text" pieces are hung in the classroom for the children to share and retell with each other.

4. Individual reading

   a. Copies of the book are made available in the book corner so children can revisit the story on their own.

5. Dramatic play

   a. Hen, cat, pig, and dog puppets are placed in the dramatic play area so children can act out the story.

Not only do these *Little Red Hen* learning activities address early literacy development (retelling a story, story sense, personal connections to text), but they address skills in other domains as well:

- Physical Well-Being and Motor Development
  - Physical movement through dramatic play
  - Fine motor development through drawing, cutting, painting, gluing
- Social Development
  - Cooperating, taking turns
  - Interacting with teachers and peers
- Language and Communication Development
  - Understanding word meaning, acquisition of new vocabulary
  - Listening, asking and answering questions
  - Communicating ideas and thoughts
- Cognitive Development and General Knowledge
  - Learning sequencing skills
  - Understanding concepts of time
  - Understanding that certain behaviors have consequences

Source: Cappelloni, 2011.

Resource 4.3 Creative Play Center

Creative play centers, dramatic play, and playhouse areas enable children to pretend, role-play, problem solve, negotiate, cooperate, make choices, plan, and act out everyday, real-life experiences. Play that evolves through these situations provides opportunities to rehearse different roles, strengthens social competencies and peer interactions, and enables children to express their thoughts, feelings, and emotions. Communication skills are tapped into as children converse with and listen to their peers as they play. Reading and writing are incorporated as children create signs, make lists, write and read menus, take orders, pay cashiers, write and deliver letters, and take notes. Some ideas for real-life settings to be used as creative play centers in the classroom include

- post office
- grocery store
- restaurant
- office
- school
- home

Resource 4.4 Scientific Inquiry Through the Five Senses

Scientific inquiry in preschool allows young children hands-on opportunities to explore, experiment, investigate, discover, and understand the physical world around them through the use of their senses. What better way to provide these learning experiences than through a unit on the five senses? You will discover that studying the five senses also accommodates many different learning styles by incorporating all of the multiple intelligences.

Scientific Inquiry through the Five Senses

Application of the Dimensions of Early Learning and Development in a curricular unit on The Five Senses	Physical Well-Being and Motor Development: Learning about our bodies, how they function, and how to keep them healthy	Social Development: Cooperating, taking turns, sharing	Emotional Development: Understanding different perspectives, expressing feelings and personal ideas	Approaches Toward Learning: Curiosity, inquiry, exploration, experiment, discovery	Emerging Literacy Development: Shared reading, guided reading, independent reading, writing responses	Language and Communication Development: Oral language development, sharing thoughts and ideas, listening, learning new vocabulary and word meanings	Cognitive Development and General Knowledge: Learning about the science of the human body
Touch	Fine motor: finger painting	Sharing "touch picture" materials	Question: Why do I like to touch these things?	Discovering sense of touch: "touch" pictures	Read *My Five Senses and Lucy's Picture*; illustrate and label *"things I like to touch"*	Create *touch rhymes*	Learning about sense of touch
Taste	Discussing healthy bodies; nutrition	Cooperating at taste stations	Question: What do the tastes remind me of?	Discovering sense of taste: "taste test"	Read *Six Silly Eaters*; write/illustrate *"things I like to taste"*	Sing a song about *food*	Learning about sense of taste and taste buds

Application of the Dimensions of Early Learning and Development in a curricular unit on The Five Senses	Physical Well-Being and Motor Development: Learning about our bodies, how they function, and how to keep them healthy	Social Development: Cooperating, taking turns, sharing	Emotional Development: Understanding different perspectives, expressing feelings and personal ideas	Approaches Toward Learning: Curiosity, inquiry, exploration, experiment, discovery	Emerging Literacy Development: Shared reading, guided reading, independent reading, writing responses	Language and Communication Development: Oral language development, sharing thoughts and ideas, listening, learning new vocabulary and word meanings	Cognitive Development and General Knowledge: Learning about the science of the human body
Sound	Fine motor: pouring seeds in sound cans	Sharing musical instruments and collaborating making sound cans	Question: What would it be like if I couldn't hear?	Discovering sense of hearing: "sound cans"	Read *Sound*; Write/illustrate "things I like to hear"	Listening to books on tapes	Learning about sense of hearing
Smell	Fine motor: crushing small herbs for smelling	Take turns in smell stations	Question: What do these smells make me think of?	Discovering sense of smell: "smell stations"	Write/illustrate "things I like to smell"; read *Smell*	Create a *smell* poem	Learning about sense of smell, learning about relationship between smell and taste: apple experiment
Sight	Fine motor: "reading" braille with fingers	Play color/ shape bingo; Guided "blind" walk with partner	Question: What would it be like if I couldn't see?	Discovering sense of sight: magnification experiment	Read *Sense Suspense* and *A Guide Dog Puppy Grows Up*	*I Spy* book and game	Learning about sense of sight; popcorn experiment—how it integrates all senses

Resource 4.5 Kindergarten Common Core Content Standards: Kindergarten Mathematics

Counting and Cardinality

Know number names and the count sequence.

- **K.CC.1.** Count to 100 by ones and by tens.
- **K.CC.2.** Count forward beginning from a given number within the known sequence (instead of having to begin at 1).
- **K.CC.3.** Write numbers from 0 to 20. Represent a number of objects with a written numeral 0–20 (with 0 representing a count of no objects).

Count to tell the number of objects.

- **K.CC.4.** Understand the relationship between numbers and quantities; connect counting to cardinality.
  - o When counting objects, say the number names in the standard order, pairing each object with one and only one number name and each number name with one and only one object.
  - o Understand that the last number name said tells the number of objects counted. The number of objects is the same regardless of their arrangement or the order in which they were counted.
  - o Understand that each successive number name refers to a quantity that is one larger.
- **K.CC.5.** Count to answer "how many?" questions about as many as 20 things arranged in a line, a rectangular array, or a circle, or as many as 10 things in a scattered configuration; given a number from 1–20, count out that many objects.

Compare numbers.

- **K.CC.6.** Identify whether the number of objects in one group is greater than, less than, or equal to the number of objects in another group (e.g., by using matching and counting strategies). (This includes groups with up to ten objects.)
- **K.CC.7.** Compare two numbers between 1 and 10 presented as written numerals.

Operations and Algebraic Thinking

Understand addition as putting together and adding to, and understand subtraction as taking apart and taking from.

- **K.OA.1.** Represent addition and subtraction with objects, fingers, mental images, drawings (Drawings need not show details, but should show the mathematics in the problem. [This applies wherever drawings are mentioned in the Standards.]), sounds (e.g., claps), acting out situations, verbal explanations, expressions, or equations.
- **K.OA.2.** Solve addition and subtraction word problems, and add and subtract within 10, e.g., by using objects or drawings to represent the problem.
- **K.OA.3.** Decompose numbers less than or equal to 10 into pairs in more than one way, e.g., by using objects or drawings, and record each decomposition by a drawing or equation (e.g., $5 = 2 + 3$ and $5 = 4 + 1$).

- **K.OA.4.** For any number from 1 to 9, find the number that makes 10 when added to the given number, e.g., by using objects or drawings, and record the answer with a drawing or equation.
- **K.OA.5.** Fluently add and subtract within 5.

Number and Operations in Base Ten

Work with numbers 11–19 to gain foundations for place value.

- **K.NBT.1.** Compose and decompose numbers from 11 to 19 into ten ones and some further ones, e.g., by using objects or drawings, and record each composition or decomposition by a drawing or equation (such as $18 = 10 + 8$); understand that these numbers are composed of ten ones and one, two, three, four, five, six, seven, eight, or nine ones.

Measurement and Data

Describe and compare measurable attributes.

- **K.MD.1.** Describe measurable attributes of objects, such as length or weight. Describe several measurable attributes of a single object.
- **K.MD.2.** Directly compare two objects with a measurable attribute in common, to see which object has "more of"/"less of" the attribute, and describe the difference. *For example, directly compare the heights of two children and describe one child as taller/shorter.*

Classify objects and count the number of objects in each category.

- **K.MD.3.** Classify objects into given categories; count the numbers of objects in each category and sort the categories by count. Limit category counts to be less than or equal to 10.

Geometry

Identify and describe shapes (squares, circles, triangles, rectangles, hexagons, cubes, cones, cylinders, and spheres).

- **K.G.1.** Describe objects in the environment using names of shapes, and describe the relative positions of these objects using terms such as *above, below, beside, in front of, behind,* and *next to.*
- **K.G.2.** Correctly name shapes regardless of their orientations or overall size.
- **K.G.3.** Identify shapes as two-dimensional (lying in a plane, "flat") or three-dimensional ("solid").

Analyze, compare, create, and compose shapes.

- **K.G.4.** Analyze and compare two- and three-dimensional shapes, in different sizes and orientations, using informal language to describe their similarities, differences, parts (e.g., number of sides and vertices/"corners") and other attributes (e.g., having sides of equal length).

(Continued)

(Continued)

- **K.G.5.** Model shapes in the world by building shapes from components (e.g., sticks and clay balls) and drawing shapes.
- **K.G.6.** Compose simple shapes to form larger shapes. *For example, "Can you join these two triangles with full sides touching to make a rectangle?"*

Resource 4.6   Kindergarten Common Core Content Standards: Kindergarten English Language Arts

Reading: Literature

Key Ideas and Details

- **RL.K.1.** With prompting and support, ask and answer questions about key details in a text.
- **RL.K.2.** With prompting and support, retell familiar stories, including key details.
- **RL.K.3.** With prompting and support, identify characters, settings, and major events in a story.

Craft and Structure

- **RL.K.4.** Ask and answer questions about unknown words in a text.
- **RL.K.5.** Recognize common types of texts (e.g., storybooks, poems).
- **RL.K.6.** With prompting and support, name the author and illustrator of a story and define the role of each in telling the story.

Integration of Knowledge and Ideas

- **RL.K.7.** With prompting and support, describe the relationship between illustrations and the story in which they appear (e.g., what moment in a story an illustration depicts).
- **RL.K.8.** (Not applicable to literature)
- **RL.K.9.** With prompting and support, compare and contrast the adventures and experiences of characters in familiar stories.

Range of Reading and Level of Text Complexity

- **RL.K.10.** Actively engage in group reading activities with purpose and understanding.

Reading: Informational Text

Key Ideas and Details

- **RI.K.1.** With prompting and support, ask and answer questions about key details in a text.

- **RI.K.2.** With prompting and support, identify the main topic and retell key details of a text.
- **RI.K.3.** With prompting and support, describe the connection between two individuals, events, ideas, or pieces of information in a text.

Craft and Structure

- **RI.K.4.** With prompting and support, ask and answer questions about unknown words in a text.
- **RI.K.5.** Identify the front cover, back cover, and title page of a book.
- **RI.K.6.** Name the author and illustrator of a text and define the role of each in presenting the ideas or information in a text.

Integration of Knowledge and Ideas

- **RI.K.7.** With prompting and support, describe the relationship between illustrations and the text in which they appear (e.g., what person, place, thing, or idea in the text an illustration depicts).
- **RI.K.8.** With prompting and support, identify the reasons an author gives to support points in a text.
- **RI.K.9.** With prompting and support, identify basic similarities in and differences between two texts on the same topic (e.g., in illustrations, descriptions, or procedures).

Range of Reading and Level of Text Complexity

- **RI.K.10.** Actively engage in group reading activities with purpose and understanding.

Reading: Foundational Skills

Print Concepts

- **RF.K.1.** Demonstrate understanding of the organization and basic features of print.
  - Follow words from left to right, top to bottom, and page by page.
  - Recognize that spoken words are represented in written language by specific sequences of letters.
  - Understand that words are separated by spaces in print.
  - Recognize and name all upper- and lowercase letters of the alphabet.

Phonological Awareness

- **RF.K.2.** Demonstrate understanding of spoken words, syllables, and sounds (phonemes).
  - Recognize and produce rhyming words.
  - Count, pronounce, blend, and segment syllables in spoken words.
  - Blend and segment onsets and rimes of single-syllable spoken words.
  - Isolate and pronounce the initial, medial vowel, and final sounds (phonemes) in three-phoneme (consonant-vowel-consonant, or CVC) words. Words, syllables, or phonemes written in /slashes/ refer to their pronunciation or phonology. Thus,

(Continued)

(Continued)

/CVC/ is a word with three phonemes regardless of the number of letters in the spelling of the word. (This does not include CVCs ending with /l/, /r/, or /x/.)

o Add or substitute individual sounds (phonemes) in simple, one-syllable words to make new words.

Phonics and Word Recognition

- **RF.K.3.** Know and apply grade-level phonics and word analysis skills in decoding words.
  - o Demonstrate basic knowledge of letter-sound correspondences by producing the primary or most frequent sound for each consonant.
  - o Associate the long and short sounds with the common spellings (graphemes) for the five major vowels.
  - o Read common high-frequency words by sight (e.g., *the, of, to, you, she, my, is, are, do, does*).
  - o Distinguish between similarly spelled words by identifying the sounds of the letters that differ.

Fluency

- **RF.K.4.** Read emergent-reader texts with purpose and understanding.

Writing

Text Types and Purposes

- **W.K.1.** Use a combination of drawing, dictating, and writing to compose opinion pieces in which they tell a reader the topic or the name of the book they are writing about and state an opinion or preference about the topic or book (e.g., *My favorite book is . . .*).
- **W.K.2.** Use a combination of drawing, dictating, and writing to compose informative/explanatory texts in which they name what they are writing about and supply some information about the topic.
- **W.K.3.** Use a combination of drawing, dictating, and writing to narrate a single event or several loosely linked events, tell about the events in the order in which they occurred, and provide a reaction to what happened.

Production and Distribution of Writing

- **W.K.4.** (Begins in grade 3)
- **W.K.5.** With guidance and support from adults, respond to questions and suggestions from peers and add details to strengthen writing as needed.
- **W.K.6.** With guidance and support from adults, explore a variety of digital tools to produce and publish writing, including in collaboration with peers.

Research to Build and Present Knowledge

- **W.K.7.** Participate in shared research and writing projects (e.g., explore a number of books by a favorite author and express opinions about them).

- **W.K.8.** With guidance and support from adults, recall information from experiences or gather information from provided sources to answer a question.

Speaking and Listening

Comprehension and Collaboration

- **SL.K.1.** Participate in collaborative conversations with diverse partners about *kindergarten topics and texts* with peers and adults in small and larger groups.
    - o Follow agreed-upon rules for discussions (e.g., listening to others and taking turns speaking about the topics and texts under discussion).
    - o Continue a conversation through multiple exchanges.
- **SL.K.2.** Confirm understanding of a text read aloud or information presented orally or through other media by asking and answering questions about key details and requesting clarification if something is not understood.
- **SL.K.3.** Ask and answer questions in order to seek help, get information, or clarify something that is not understood.

Presentation of Knowledge and Ideas

- **SL.K.4.** Describe familiar people, places, things, and events and, with prompting and support, provide additional detail.
- **SL.K.5.** Add drawings or other visual displays to descriptions as desired to provide additional detail.
- **SL.K.6.** Speak audibly and express thoughts, feelings, and ideas clearly.

Language

Conventions of Standard English

- **L.K.1.** Demonstrate command of the conventions of standard English grammar and usage when writing or speaking.
    - o Print many upper- and lowercase letters.
    - o Use frequently occurring nouns and verbs.
    - o Form regular plural nouns orally by adding /s/ or /es/ (e.g., *dog, dogs; wish, wishes*).
    - o Understand and use question words (interrogatives) (e.g., *who, what, where, when, why, how*).
    - o Use the most frequently occurring prepositions (e.g., *to, from, in, out, on, off, for, of, by, with*).
    - o Produce and expand complete sentences in shared language activities.
- **L.K.2.** Demonstrate command of the conventions of standard English capitalization, punctuation, and spelling when writing.
    - o Capitalize the first word in a sentence and the pronoun *I*.
    - o Recognize and name end punctuation.
    - o Write a letter or letters for most consonant and short-vowel sounds (phonemes).
    - o Spell simple words phonetically, drawing on knowledge of sound-letter relationships.

(Continued)

(Continued)

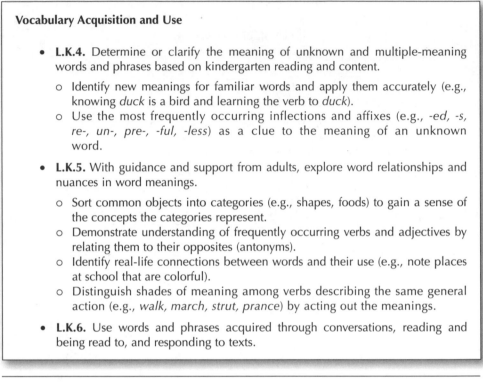

Vocabulary Acquisition and Use

- **L.K.4.** Determine or clarify the meaning of unknown and multiple-meaning words and phrases based on kindergarten reading and content.
  - o Identify new meanings for familiar words and apply them accurately (e.g., knowing *duck* is a bird and learning the verb to *duck*).
  - o Use the most frequently occurring inflections and affixes (e.g., *-ed, -s, re-, un-, pre-, -ful, -less*) as a clue to the meaning of an unknown word.
- **L.K.5.** With guidance and support from adults, explore word relationships and nuances in word meanings.
  - o Sort common objects into categories (e.g., shapes, foods) to gain a sense of the concepts the categories represent.
  - o Demonstrate understanding of frequently occurring verbs and adjectives by relating them to their opposites (antonyms).
  - o Identify real-life connections between words and their use (e.g., note places at school that are colorful).
  - o Distinguish shades of meaning among verbs describing the same general action (e.g., *walk, march, strut, prance*) by acting out the meanings.
- **L.K.6.** Use words and phrases acquired through conversations, reading and being read to, and responding to texts.

Source: http://www.corestandards.org/the-standards/english-language-arts-standards. © Copyright 2010. National Governors Association Center for Best Practices and Council of Chief State School Officers. All rights reserved.

CONCLUSION

Research findings suggest that children who begin kindergarten with certain resources are at a developmental advantage. These advantages are also sustainable over time. Early childhood educational experiences are formative for a child's later developing years. Young children, especially during the first five years of life, have an impressive learning capacity, and the nurturing of those capacities is critical for their educational achievements in following years. The quality of the preschool's classroom environment contributes to a child's ability to acquire important readiness skills. The environment must support the learning goals and the curriculum and be conducive to children's learning and development in all domains. Chapter 5 will discuss the learning environment in its totality— the physical environment, the emotional climate, and the climate of culturally responsive teaching.

PROFESSIONAL DEVELOPMENT DISCUSSION GUIDE

1. Deepen Your Thinking
    a. Choose one or more of these individual inquiry questions for group discussion:
        1. Readiness for school is dependent not only on the particular skills, abilities, characteristics, and knowledge that the individual child brings to school but also on the readiness of the kindergarten classroom and school in which they enroll, suggesting that schools must be ready for all children (Kagan et al., 1995; NAEYC, 2003, 2009; NEGP, 1993; Shore, 1998). What exactly do you think this means? How can schools and classrooms be ready for the increasingly diverse students entering our kindergartens each year?

WHERE CAN I LEARN MORE?

California Department of Education. (2000). *Prekindergarten Learning and Development Guidelines.* Berkeley: Child Development Division, California Department of Education; Health and Education Communication Consultants.

California Department of Education. (2008). *California Preschool Learning Foundations* (Vol. 1). Sacramento: Child Development Division, California Department of Education.

California Department of Education. (2010). *California Preschool Curriculum Framework* (Vol. 1). Sacramento: Child Development Division, California Department of Education.

California Department of Education. (2010). *California Preschool Learning Foundations* (Vol. 2). Sacramento: Child Development Division, California Department of Education.

California Department of Education. (2011). *California Preschool Curriculum Framework* (Vol. 2). Sacramento: Child Development Division, California Department of Education.

Common Core Content Standards: English Language Arts and Mathematics Standards http://www.corestandards.org/

International Reading Association http://www.reading.org

National Association for the Education of Young Children (NAEYC) http://naeyc.org

National Council of Teachers of Mathematics http://www.nctm.org

5 Creating a Developmentally Appropriate Classroom Learning Environment

The quality of the classroom learning environment contributes to a child's ability to acquire academic skills (Mashburn, 2008). According to the National Education Goals Panel (NEGP), in order to optimize children's early learning and development and help children become competent and successful in school, there must be a match between the child and the child's learning environment (Shore, 1998).

Public schools today are experiencing a radical shift in the growing range of ethnic and racial groups and home languages. In 2009, almost 46 percent of public school students enrolled in prekindergarten through 12th grade were students of races/ethnicities other than white. Almost seven percent of students between the ages of five and nine spoke a language other than English at home and spoke English with difficulty (National Center for Education Statistics [NCES], 2012). In many large cities and states, "minority" students have become the majority in public schools, a trend that will soon characterize our entire country (Darling-Hammond et al., 2009, p. 106). *Culturally responsive teaching* describes practices that teachers use to succeed with a range of diverse students. In a culturally responsive classroom, the developmentally appropriate curriculum and instruction supports individual, cultural, and linguistic diversity by taking into account cultural differences in learning, differing learning styles, communication styles, values, attitudes, behaviors, language differences, gender equality, and diverse perspectives. Underlying this practice is a respect for all students and a belief in their potential as learners (Darling-Hammond et al., 2009). The *developmentally appropriate classroom learning environment* is one that supports the developmentally appropriate curriculum. This match is through the physical environment, the emotional environment, and teaching practices that support all learners with an underlying expectation that all children will learn.

Developmental psychologist Lev Vygotsky (1896–1934) conceptualized learning as a social process, suggesting that knowledge is constructed through our interactions with others (Vygotsky, 1978). Teachers can design learning environments that will encourage children to interact and learn from each other. The teacher promotes learning opportunities designed to give children hands-on, experiential, and activity-based opportunities to observe, explore, engage in, invent, and discover in areas of interest to them and with opportunities for student choice. The teacher's role can be conceptualized as an assistant to students in this social system (Darling-Hammond et al., 2009, p. 129).

The *physical* developmentally appropriate classroom learning environment is both safe and accessible to all children. The environment inspires and fosters inquiry and exploration in all domains to support different learning styles and individual interests and needs. Well-organized class-rooms have been shown to reflect students' engagement, interest, active participation, and learning (Hamre & Pianta, 2007). Therefore, materials, supplies, furniture, and equipment enhance indoor and outdoor play environments to encourage imagination, discovery, invention, cooperation, and creativity, with the overarching expectation that all children will learn, grow, and succeed.

Some examples of materials in a stimulating physical environment to encourage growth and learning in all domains are included below.

EARLY LITERACY, LANGUAGE, AND COMMUNICATION

For this domain, many materials can be used, including different kinds of paper for writing and art, colored markers, crayons, pencils with pencil grips, chalkboards with chalk and erasers, and whiteboards with dry-erase pens and erasers. A library corner with books of all kinds (i.e., concept books, rhyming, fairy tales, nonfiction informational text, fiction) is a must (containing a collection of big books and other read-aloud books) as well as a writing center, a music center with musical instruments and CDs, and a listening center with books on tape.

PHYSICAL MOTOR DEVELOPMENT

Encouraging physical motor development includes the use of equipment and materials for two subgroups: large motor and sensorimotor skills (large blocks, balls, bikes, scooters, mats, climbing structures, jump ropes, hula hoops, cones, bean bags, ramps, sandbox, water table, parachutes, etc.) and fine motor skills (Legos, small blocks, scissors, glue sticks, clay, sewing cards, jacks, spray bottles, paint brushes, chalk, tweezers, tongs, basters, eye droppers, clothes pins, hole punches, etc.).

SOCIAL AND EMOTIONAL DEVELOPMENT

Social and emotional development are enhanced through a creative/dramatic play area with props and materials to play store, home, office, school, restaurant, post office and role-play other everyday experiences; an art center with a wide assortment of materials available for self-expression and creativity; and board games (for two or more players, including memory games and bingo).

COGNITIVE DEVELOPMENT AND
GENERAL KNOWLEDGE

Some examples of materials used to stimulate cognitive development and general knowledge include many different kinds of puzzles; concept and nonfiction books; blocks of various kinds and sizes; objects to sort, order, count, and make patterns with; math manipulatives, and a science center with live insects, fish, and animals and plants, rocks, and shells.

Introducing new materials stimulates interest and invites exploration in new areas. Responding to children's interests, accommodating and challenging their growing abilities, and presenting them with more complex activities and tasks will provide children with opportunities to learn and ensure their continued development. Child-focused learning environments—those in which children play an instrumental role in their choice of learning activities and in which teachers create learning experiences that are responsive to children's interests—have been shown to increase children's positive feelings, motivation, and engagement in school (Hamre & Pianta, 2007).

THE EMOTIONALLY SAFE
CLASSROOM ENVIRONMENT

An *emotionally safe classroom environment* is one that promotes respect, caring, acceptance, and compassion for all children. Since emotions have an impact on learning and emotions influence our ability to process information, it is critical for teachers to create a positive, emotionally safe classroom environment for children's optimal learning, growth, and expression. Hamre and Pianta (2007) describe a positive classroom climate as one in which children experience warm, caring relationships with teachers and peers, feel secure and competent, and enjoy the time they spend in school. Children who are more motivated and experience positive adult and peer relationships during their early years in school have been shown to be successful both socially and academically in subsequent years (Darling-Hammond et al., 2009; Hamre & Pianta, 2007).

It is important for teachers to listen to their students and respond to their concerns, needs, and feelings with sensitivity and warmth. Teachers can help children recognize, understand, manage, and express their feelings; handle difficult situations and frustrations; and resolve a problem or a conflict. The emotionally safe classroom is a supportive and safe place for children to talk about their feelings, to become aware of others' feelings and empathize with others, to learn effective ways of resolving conflict, and to accept new challenges (Darling-Hammond et al., 2009).

Teachers can create and foster a *community of learners* (National Association for the Education of Young Children [NAEYC], 2009, p. 16), which supports the needs of all children to learn, grow, and develop through positive, caring relationships between teachers and children and between all children. This community of learners is inclusive of all children, regardless of home language, culture, or special needs. Every child is respected and valued and has a voice, and teachers are responsive and sensitive in order to ensure that children feel safe to explore and engage in learning.

CONCLUSION

The developmentally appropriate classroom learning environment promotes caring, respect, and inclusiveness. It is safe and accessible to all children. The environment emphasizes active learning and authentic tasks through materials, equipment, and opportunities designed for exploration, creativity, inquiry, and the acquisition of knowledge.

PROFESSIONAL DEVELOPMENT DISCUSSION GUIDE

1. Deepen Your Thinking:
   a. Choose one or more of these individual inquiry topics for group discussion:
      i. What are some ways you can create a safe and exciting learning environment by moving things around, without having to buy any new furniture?
      ii. How can you create a fun and inviting writing center with materials that will encourage children to illustrate and write?
      iii. How can you create an exciting and engaging art center with recyclable materials?

WHERE CAN I LEARN MORE?

EduCLIME http://www.educlime.com

Handwriting Without Tears http://www.hwtears.com/hwt

Pocket Full of Therapy http://www.pfot.com

INSTA-LEARN http://www.insta-learn.com

6 Assessment of Young Children

A ssessments in early childhood education are primarily used for evalu- ating programs, monitoring trends and school accountability, identi- fying special needs, and supporting learning (Bowman, Donovan, & Burns, 2001). The purpose of this chapter is to discuss how assessment supports and promotes learning and development and guides instruction.

The overall goal of assessing young children in the preschool setting is to provide a means by which an individual child's skills, abilities, and/or traits can be identified. By following a structured, developmentally appro- priate, ongoing, and systematic approach to assessment and by focusing on each child's progress toward meeting certain learning goals, assess- ment results provide important information to preschool teachers, kinder- garten teachers, and families about the individual child's competencies and his or her readiness for school.

The National Association for the Education of Young Children (NAEYC) asserts that "assessment of children's development and learning is essential for teachers and programs in order to plan, implement, and evaluate the effectiveness of the classroom experiences they provide" (NAEYC, 2009, p. 22). The NAEYC claims that assessments will be helpful in informing instruction, however, only if they are aligned with and support instruc- tional goals and teaching activities. In developmentally appropriate prac- tice, the experiences and the assessments are linked and aligned so that *what is being taught is being assessed,* and the assessment results inform fur- ther instruction. The NAEYC calls for "ongoing, strategic, and purposeful" assessment of young children's progress and achievements (2009, p. 22).

Assessment helps educators monitor children's progress toward desired goals and may even identify areas that may be of concern. Assessment data inform and drive future instruction—by revealing both what children know and can do and by identifying areas in which children need further develop- ment. Teachers use assessment data for instructional planning geared toward meeting the needs of individual students. Determining what chil- dren already know and are able to do is a necessary component of develop- ing and enhancing curricular activities to meet the emerging needs of young students and help them reach desired learning goals.

Assessing children in their natural classroom environment over a period of time is referred to by Pianta and Howes as "authentic child assessment" (2009, p. 113). The familiar classroom setting with familiar classroom teachers provides the child with a comfortable and normal set- ting for completing assessment tasks that the child is already familiar with. These researchers describe assessment as

a collaborative process that should take place over time and in natu- ral settings. It involves observing, recording, and documenting data about children as they interact with the world around them. Assessment results of young children can be affected by many factors and should be viewed as an emerging picture of a child's learning and development. (Pianta & Howes, 2009, p. 115)

Assessment results provide opportunities to share information with students' families, providing an "emerging" picture of their child's readiness on an ongoing basis (Pianta & Howes, 2009, p. 114). Since parents are believed by many to be a child's first and most important teachers, discussing a child's progress, as demonstrated through assessment results, enables teachers to help families implement strategies at home for enhancing further growth and development. Alternatively, assessments can help teachers discover when a child has particular strengths in areas that can be encouraged and developed even further.

Preschool assessments administered at the end of the school year will be particularly useful to kindergarten teachers. The results will provide them with a snapshot of each child's abilities and skills in a number of areas. Although much growth and development occur between the last preschool assessment and the first day of kindergarten, the preschool assessment results give kindergarten teachers an initial starting point in understanding their incoming students' abilities. These results should help prevent any *big* surprises for kindergarten teachers when kindergarten first begins. Once kindergarten has begun, most kindergarten teachers assess their new students with school-adopted assessments for the purpose of identifying abilities and competencies and guiding differentiated instruction.

Are assessments necessary, appropriate, fair, and unbiased? Assessments of preschool age children can be challenging and must be approached cautiously. Pianta and Howes suggest that preschool-age children's learning is "sporadic and explosive" and that young children grow and change rapidly. They suggest that assessment must be "ongoing, developmentally appropriate, administered cautiously, and broadly interpreted" (2009, p. 118.) The NAEYC suggests that assessment of young children is challenging because the way in which they learn and develop is embedded within the specific linguistic and cultural contexts in which they live (NAEYC, 2009). The increasing cultural and linguistic diversity as well as the wide range of verbal abilities of young children in early childhood educational programs raise concerns regarding many assessment's English-only formats (Snow, 2011).

Given that kindergarten readiness is a composite of skills and abilities across all domains of early learning and development, it is important to assess children in all domains and in different ways. This integrated approach to assessment takes into consideration the whole child and uses multiple sources of data (Pianta & Howes, 2009). Further, children of this age develop skills and abilities in all domains simultaneously, but not at the same rate. The Gesell Institute of Child Development suggests that child development during these early years is "fluid and variable and involves many ups-and-downs, including behavior that may look like set-backs or regression" (Gesell Institute of Child Development, 2011, p. 4).

The NAEYC promotes the use of developmentally (including culturally and linguistically) appropriate assessments of young children for the pur-pose of improving instruction and programs. The NAEYC and National Association of Early Childhood Specialists in State Departments of Education (NAECS/SDE) 2003 position statement on curriculum, instruction, and assessment emphasizes the need for an integrated system, aligning assess-ments with curriculum and instruction (Snow, 2011). The Gesell Institute reminds educators that assessments and screening instruments should not be used to diagnose or label a child, that they should be sensitive to cultural differences, and that they should view screening instruments as *only one* part of a comprehensive and integrated assessment system. While there is gen-eral consensus among early childhood educators that the use of assessments can contribute to improving and guiding instruction, just how and what young children should be assessed on is more debatable.

First, have a clear understanding of what you are trying to evaluate and what you plan to do with the results. Second, identify the following: What specific skills or abilities do you want to assess in each child? Which assessment measures will you use to seek that information? What will you do with the assessment results (i.e., how will they be used to inform and drive future instruction or to report to families and teachers)? Finally, keep in mind that the methods of assessment need to be appropriate for the developmental stages and experiences of young learners and must recog-nize individual variation in learners and allow children to demonstrate their competencies in all domains in many different ways (NAEYC, 2009).

As a teacher, you will be interested to learn where each student falls on a continuum of learning. Young children's learning tends to go through a series of phases as they assimilate and accommodate new information, make connections, and create new knowledge. Informal assessments (as opposed to formal, standardized testing) can be administered at any point throughout the year, thereby allowing you to assess children's competen-cies, reflect on the results, and adjust or modify your instruction to match the developing nature of children's learning.

Appropriate informal assessment methods for young children in the preschool classroom can include teachers' focused observations of children playing, teachers' observations of children's performance-based authentic assessments and tasks, checklists, interviews with children, anecdotal notes, and collections of children's work over time. Keep a folder for each child with work samples, records, assessments, and notes. Collectively, these informal assessments will form a portfolio of the child, capturing and demonstrating his or her skills, interests, strengths, and knowledge. In this way, assessments will be based on multiple sources collected over a long period of time, reflecting a wide range of learning experiences from more than one observer and from more than one method. The following are commonly used assessment methods in the preschool environment:

- Performance-based or *authentic* assessments
  - These seek to measure a student's ability to perform or complete a task, demonstrating real competencies and revealing what they know and are able to do. They focus on the assessment of concrete, observable behaviors on real tasks that are part of the child's regular classroom activities and experiences in the natural classroom setting (Bowman et al., 2001; Jonson, Cappelloni, & Niesyn, 2011).
- Classroom observations and anecdotal notes
  - Careful, systematic observation is a critical tool for early assessment of student behavior, knowledge, and abilities. The notes you take become an important tool for understanding the individual child's strengths and weaknesses.
    - In the beginning of the year, create a logbook to maintain a record of your observations. You may find it handy as you move about the classroom to carry a pad of sticky notes in your pocket to jot down observations, which can later be recorded in the logbook under the appropriate child's name. Be sure to check off names to ensure that you observe every student. Some teachers select a target student or students for the day. This strategy allows you to observe a single student in a wide array of contexts. By doing this, you will gain important information about your students that may otherwise go unnoticed and that you will want to share during teacher-family conferences.
    - Make a number of observations over time. One-shot observations are unreliable indicators of student stability or growth. By looking at children in many different learning situations and settings and on different occasions, you will be able to detect patterns, document growth, and identify areas that need to be addressed. Focus on the whole child—socially, emotionally, physically, and academically. Learn to document a child's skills, accomplishments, and abilities as the child participates in routine classroom activities and interacts with peers, adults, and materials.

- Know what you are looking for. Don't try to take it all in.
- Record exactly what you see or exactly what students do. Avoid temptations to infer, insinuate, judge, diagnose, or inflate assessment results based on your prior knowledge of the student and his or her abilities. Try to be objective. Separate your emotions from the assessment process.
- Having all teachers observe all children at different points in time will bring a greater collective picture of the child (Jonson et al., 2011).

- Interviews
  o Individual interviews with children will give you valuable information. Understanding your students from their perspective gives you greater insight and a more complete picture of each individual child. Questions can range from "Who are your friends at school?" and "What do you like best about school?" to "Count as far as you can go starting from 1," or "Let me hear you say the alphabet."

There are many assessments available for use in the early childhood setting. Referred to as *assessment instruments, tools, screenings,* or *tests,* these include different observational systems, checklists, completion of tasks, systems for collecting portfolios, and family and teacher questionnaires. Assessments vary as to what they are evaluating and measuring. They fall under different categories, such as *Observation Tools, Screening Tools, Behavior and Social/Emotional Development, Speech and Language, Readiness Assessments,* and *Motor/Sensory Assessments.* Some are described as providing systematic methods for observing, recording, and evaluating each child's progress; some claim to help teachers identify what children are learning, what they are beginning to master, and what they still need to work on; and some claim to identify children who may need additional assessments and support in order to perform successfully in school. The technicalities of assessments vary in a number of ways: qualification requirements of the assessor, age range of the child being assessed, time required for test completion, individual or group administration, format, standardization (norm-referenced, tested for validity, and reliability), versions in Spanish for children for whom Spanish is their primary language (see the NAEYC position statement on screening English language learners, 2009), scores and interpretation, and scoring method options. Most current editions of assessments have been revised to be more culturally, gender, and linguistically sensitive and responsive to all young children (Pearson Early Childhood Assessments, 2012).

Assessments differ in what they are attempting to measure. Some choose a specific area within a developmental domain, while other assessments attempt to address a child's abilities across all domains of early learning and development. Therefore, the child's skills, abilities, and characteristics in all developmental domains (physical/motor, social, emotional, approaches toward learning, language and communication, emerging literacy, and cognitive development and general knowledge) should be assessed to get a complete profile of the individual child. The benefits of assessment results serve many purposes, including helping teachers individualize instruction, communicate with families more effectively, monitor developmental progress, pinpoint children's strengths and weaknesses, promote early identification and focus intervention strategies, inform curriculum and instruction planning, lay the groundwork for future achievement, and increase positive outcomes (Pearson Early Childhood Assessment, 2012).

What do you want to measure in each domain? Some examples of commonly measured indicators for each domain of early learning and development might include the following:

- Physical/Motor Development
  - Performs self-help skills and takes care of personal needs
    - Buttons, puts on, and takes off coat; puts on shoes; uses bathroom independently; cleans up after playing; eats and cleans up independently
  - Gross motor skills (balance and gross-motor planning)
    - Walks, runs, jumps, hops, skips, balances on one foot, throws, catches, walks backwards and sideways
  - Visual motor and visual discrimination skills
    - Traces and copies forms (circle, cross, square, triangle, diamond)
  - Fine motor skills
    - Manipulates small objects, sewing, cutting
- Emerging Literacy Development
  - Letter identification
    - Identifies upper- and lowercase letters
  - Letter-sound correspondence
    - Knows letter sounds
  - Writes letters of the alphabet
  - Writes own name
  - Draws, scribbles, or writes to express meaning
  - Understands story sense
  - Developing phonemic awareness: rhyming, sound isolation (beginning sound), segmenting (sentences and syllables)

- Cognitive Development and General Knowledge (concept knowledge)
  - Number identification
    - Identifies the numbers to 10
    - Counts to . . .
    - Writes numbers to . . .
  - Identifies body parts
  - Draws a complete person with body parts
  - Demonstrates understanding of directional, positional, and quantitative concepts
  - Identifies colors and basic geometric shapes
  - Gives personal data
    - First and last name, age, family members' names, favorite story
  - Sorts, orders, and groups objects
  - Sequences events in time
  - Makes associations
  - Copies or extends a simple pattern

The social, emotional, approaches toward learning, and language and communication domains are more difficult to assess, since they are more abstract than academic abilities. These domains are more easily measured through informal assessments, particularly through observation. Observational measures might include some form of checklist or rating scale during a certain block of time on a typical classroom day through normal preschool activities in which the child both works alone and interacts with others. These observations are best done over time, since one attempt may not give a true picture of the child's usual behavior. Be aware, however, that observations are subject to the observer's own interpretations. The *assessor* (the teacher giving the assessment) needs to be sensitive to the child's mood, feelings, and attention at the time of the assessment. The child could be very distracted by something else at the time. The assessor may even be unintentionally assisting the child in completing tasks.

For the social, emotional, approaches toward learning, and language and communication domains, observation checklist items might include assessing the extent to which a child does the following:

- Language/Communication Development
  - Answers simple questions
  - Asks questions
  - Engages in conversations with adults and other children
  - Names and identifies objects
  - Rhymes and sings
  - Listens to others speaking

- Social/Emotional Development
  - o Shows compliance with rules and authority figures
  - o Demonstrates focus and pays attention
  - o Demonstrates self-control and impulse control
  - o Follows classroom rules and two-step directions
  - o Plays and cooperates with other children
  - o Takes turns and shares
  - o Forms and maintains friendships with peers
  - o Interacts with children and adults
  - o Shows persistence in completing tasks
  - o Demonstrates independence in activities
  - o Resolves conflict in a nonaggressive manner
  - o Expresses feelings
  - o Demonstrates curiosity, enthusiasm, and engagement in learning
  - o Asks teachers for help when needed
  - o Listens to a story for 10 minutes or more

The NAEYC suggests that assessment looks not only at what the child can do independently but what the child is learning to do and can do with teacher support or peer support. Therefore, observations should be done during situations in which children participate with others or in other situations in which scaffolding is provided (NAEYC, 2009).

CONCLUSION

Assessment in and of itself is of limited value in the absence of instructional guidance, which puts into practice the information learned through the assessment results (Bowman et al., 2001). The goal of all assessment should be to inform teachers of children's growing abilities and progress. Assessment results should be used for the purposes of

- establishing goals to guide objectives to improve skills and abilities,
- guiding instruction in planning curriculum and learning activities in order to improve teaching,
- monitoring progress,
- providing intervention,
- determining whether further assessment is warranted, and
- communicating with families.

Assessments inform teachers and families of the child's abilities, skills, and characteristics in the classroom and are used to support learning and drive instructional choices and practices. Enough time between assessments is needed to build strengths and measure children's growth and achievement over time. Assessments should be done frequently and in a timely manner, coordinated with family conferences. It is recommended, therefore, that assessment in the late fall provide a baseline. Another assessment in winter will provide time for the child to continue making progress. The spring assessment will enable the child to demonstrate a year of growth and will provide important benchmarks for the start of kindergarten.

Children's performance on tasks and skills should reflect their growth toward specific learning goals. Assessment results help teachers more effectively prepare their students for kindergarten readiness. It is important to keep in mind that, as NAEYC reminds us, important decisions such as enrollment or placement should never be made on the basis of results from a single assessment or screening instrument but should be based on multiple sources of information (NAEYC, 2009).

While this author does not endorse any particular standardized assessments, kindergarten readiness tests, developmental screening tests, diagnostic assessments for four- or five-year-olds, or other screening instruments or tests, reviews of a variety of these screening instruments can be found. Meisels articulately cautions the use of and the limitations of readiness tests:

> Not only do children, especially young children, acquire skills at different rates and in different ways, but they are also exquisitely sensitive to the opportunity to learn. If a child has not been taught his or her colors or shapes or has not been exposed to opportunities to acquire these skills, then that information will not be available to the child. . . . Readiness tests . . . assume a common core of learning before school; but this is unjustified. Children who do poorly on readiness tests often do well on similar assessments by the end of their kindergarten year; . . . the problem is not with the children but with the tests. (Meisels, 1999, pp. 54–55)

Although assessment results need to be interpreted cautiously (remembering that normal development in the preschool child falls within a wide range), assessments may help determine whether a child may demonstrate significant weaknesses in certain areas or may be in need of additional follow-ups, screenings, or services. Assessments can help teachers identify and target specific areas of concern. Chapter 7 includes more information about what is within a normal range of development, identifying the potential need for additional services for children with special needs, identifying children that may be at risk of falling behind or may possibly be in need of formal intervention, and recognizing what behaviors and skills may be of concern and what to do about them.

SAMPLE ASSESSMENT CHECKLISTS AND TEMPLATES

Resource 6.1   Fine Motor/Graphomotor Abilities

Skill	Date: Fall	Date: Winter	Date: Spring
Cuts with scissors			
Uses glue stick			
Sews with sewing cards			
Builds with Legos			
Manipulates other small objects			
Uses proper pencil grip			
Colors in the lines			
Traces a shape			
Copies a shape			
Draws shapes independently			
Traces numbers and letters			
Copies numbers and letters			
Writes own name			
Draws a person with head and body parts			

Resource 6.2 Color, Trace, and Draw Shapes

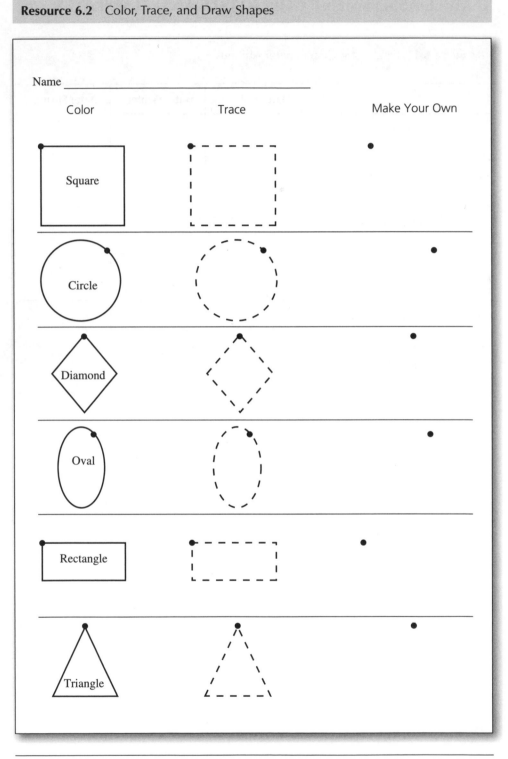

Name _____

Color	Trace	Make Your Own
Square		
Circle		
Diamond		
Oval		
Rectangle		
Triangle		

Source: Educational Software for Guiding Instruction (ESGI).

Resource 6.3 Cognitive/General Knowledge Abilities

Skill	Date: Fall	Date: Winter	Date: Spring
Orders objects			
Sorts objects by attribute			
Counts numbers to 10 or above			
Recognizes numbers to 10 or above			
Writes numbers to 10 or above			
Sequences numbers to 10 or above			
Identifies colors			
Identifies basic geometric shapes			
Knows personal data:			
Name			
Age			
Home phone			
Address			
Family members			

Resource 6.4 Numbers 1–20

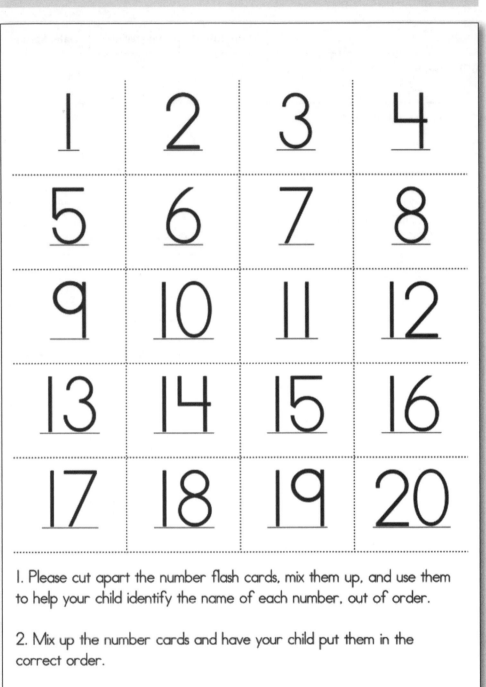

1	2	3	4
5	6	7	8
9	10	11	12
13	14	15	16
17	18	19	20

1. Please cut apart the number flash cards, mix them up, and use them to help your child identify the name of each number, out of order.

2. Mix up the number cards and have your child put them in the correct order.

Source: Educational Software for Guiding Instruction (ESGI).

Resource 6.5 Emerging Literacy Abilities

Skill	Date: Fall	Date: Winter	Date: Spring
Recites the alphabet			
Recognizes/knows names of the letters of the alphabet: lowercase			
Recognizes/knows names of the letters of the alphabet: uppercase			
Identifies letter sounds			
Identifies rhyming words			
Produces rhyming words			
Uses appropriate book handling			
Demonstrates an understanding of conventions of print			
Recognizes own written name			
Writes own name			
Writes letters of the alphabet			
Produces letter strands, words			
Reads some sight words			

Resource 6.6 Alphabet Uppercase Letters

S	R	M	K
Z	P	T	B
W	C	J	D
H	X	N	F
L	G	V	Q
Y	A	E	I
O	U		

Resource 6.7 Alphabet Lowercase Letters

Resource 6.8 Blank Assessment Template

Skill	Date: Fall	Date: Winter	Date: Spring

PROFESSIONAL DEVELOPMENT DISCUSSION GUIDE

1. Deepen Your Thinking

    a. Choose one or more of these individual inquiry topics for group discussion:

        i. What are some of the benefits of assessing children in your classroom?

        ii. What are some of your concerns regarding assessment in your preschool classroom?

        iii. Try to articulate reasonable and specific benchmarks that you would like to see children reach for each of the skills that you are assessing.

WHERE CAN I LEARN MORE?

Educational Software for Guiding Instruction (ESGI)
http://www.esgisoftware.com/ESGI/

Gesell Institute of Child Development http://www.gesellinstitute.org.

National Association for the Education of Young Children (NAEYC)
http://www.naeyc.org.

National Institute for Early Education Research http://nieer.org

Peabody Picture Vocabulary Test (4th ed.; PPVT-4) http://psychcorp.pearsonassessments
.com/HAIWEB/Cultures/en-us/Productdetail.htm?Pid=PAa30700

Pearson. (2012). *Early Childhood Assessments*. San Antonio, TX: Author.
http://psychcorp.com

Phonological Awareness Literacy Screening (PALS) http://pals.virginia.edu/

7

Addressing the Needs of Struggling Children

Preschool teachers are often the first to identify significant weaknesses, developmental delays, or signs of struggling in a child. When preschool teachers notice that a child is falling behind or simply not making progress socially, emotionally, or in language or cognitive skill acquisition, concerns arise regarding whether this child might benefit from outside testing or intervention. These "red flags" are sensed, but the pressing and challenging question is what to do next. Although it is difficult to determine the *cause* of the child's problem areas, the preschool has a responsibility to the family to help the child develop and grow to his or her fullest potential during these vital years. Although determining causes should be left to professionals through further evaluation and diagnoses, many factors might impact the child's learning, and these factors need to be addressed. They can include the following:

- Economic—Is low income or poverty impacting the child's ability to do his or her best in school or affecting his or her readiness for learning? Has there been a gap in opportunities and other advantages for this child that many other children have benefited from?
- Health—Is the child chronically sick, hungry, or tired?
- Cultural—Are there cultural differences that may be unintentionally interpreted by someone outside of that culture as a developmental lag?
- Stress—Is some recent family crisis affecting the child's mood, willingness to learn, and participation at school? Is the child experiencing divorce, separation, moving, homelessness, new household members, or the death of a family member or pet?
- Language—Is the child an English language learner who may not be fully understanding or communicating in English?

When challenging behavior occurs, it is often very difficult for teachers to determine how to respond. How severe is it? What is the frequency of the behavior? How much is the behavior impacting the child's learning and that of others? *Challenging behavior* has been described as any repeated pattern of behavior that interferes with learning or engagement in social interactions. These include physical and verbal aggression, disruptive vocal and motor behavior, destruction of property, noncompliance, withdrawal, self-injury, and disobedience. Challenging behavior during the preschool years has been shown to be one of the highest predictors of later and more serious problem behaviors, including aggression, antisocial behavior, delinquency, and substance abuse (McCabe & Frede, 2007). However, not all children who demonstrate problems and disruptive behaviors in the preschool setting maintain these over time. Teaching strategies to foster self-regulation, impulse control, problem solving, and empathy can result in children's greater social and emotional abilities as they learn new skills to assist them in developing more positive interactions with others and improve their sense of self-confidence and self-esteem.

Attention deficit/hyperactivity disorder (ADHD) is experiencing heightened attention today, as more and more young children are diagnosed and treated for ADHD. Understanding symptoms related to ADHD is important for preschool teachers. A child may demonstrate certain behaviors characteristic of ADHD, but this is never cause to diagnose the child. A list of symptoms of ADHD, published by Children and Adults with Attention Deficit/Hyperactivity Disorder (CHADD), is in Resource 7.2.

Having knowledge of early childhood development helps preschool teachers understand what is normal behavior for a four- or five-year-old child and what might not be normal. Although *normal* certainly includes a range of behaviors or characteristics, concerns arise when the teacher senses the child's behavior is out of the typical, or normal, range. Concerns may include when the child has a significant delay in at least one area of development: cognitive (ability to perceive, think, problem solve, and remember information), physical (fine, gross, and sensorimotor, vision, and hearing), communication (speech and language, including understanding and using gestures and facial expressions), social or emotional (the ability and motivation to relate to and interact with others), and/or adaptive (including self-care such as dressing, eating, and self-direction) (Marin County Office of Education, 2011).

HOW DOES THE TEACHER DETERMINE IF THERE IS A PROBLEM? WHAT HAPPENS NEXT?

There is a logical process that preschools follow to monitor learning and development in all their students in order to identify areas of challenges, weaknesses, or concern: (1) initial and ongoing assessment of all students; (2) identification of areas of challenges, weakness, or concern; (3) meeting as a professional learning community to clarify problem areas and to propose interventions; (4) implementing interventions; (5) reassessment; and (6) communicating concerns with the child's family.

Assessment

Assessment, as discussed in Chapter 6, is an ongoing and necessary process that measures children's growth over time. Teachers regularly assess children in many ways throughout the year for the purpose of monitoring children's growth, guiding further instruction, and providing individual intervention as needed. Each child is assessed in a number of areas at designated times during the year in order to measure the child's individual growth over time. The first assessment provides a reference point that subsequent assessments can be measured against. The assessment is a tool for helping teachers identify any problem areas or concerns. Assessment results and information are analyzed and compared against predetermined benchmarks in an attempt to identify those children needing additional support. If little or no growth or progress is being made, the assessment results will demonstrate that.

A word of caution: Decisions that have a major impact on the child, such as enrollment or placement, should always be based on multiple sources of relevant information (including the family's input) and should never be made on the basis of a single assessment's results. Diagnosis or labeling should also never be the result of a single form of assessment (NAEYC, 2009).

Identification of Challenges, Weaknesses, or Concerns

When a child does not make progress over time, concerns may be raised. Is the child not developmentally ready to be learning what he or she is expected to learn? Is there something going on outside of school that might be impacting learning? Is the child demonstrating a problem of some kind that has been occurring consistently? Try to explore a little further to get a better understanding of the problem. Here is an example:

Bobby was able to count to five orally, and he could count five objects accurately. He could even break down five objects and put them back together—simple addition and subtraction. Bobby could even count to ten. But could Bobby count ten objects? No, not until he was provided with instruction in counting objects with one-to-one correspondence. As soon as he learned and practiced counting objects from five to ten, touching each one as he counted, he was successful at the task. Did he recognize his numeric symbols (numbers) five through ten? No. That might be the next step for him to learn. "What does a six look like? What does a ten look like? Show me these seven objects. . . ."

Meeting as a Professional Learning Community

The core mission of the *professional learning community* is to ensure that students are learning (DuFour, 2004). The ongoing exploration of three crucial questions drives the work of the professional learning community model, which includes participation and input from *all* staff within the learning environment:

1. What do we want each student to learn?

2. How will we know when each student has learned it?

3. How will we respond when a student experiences difficulty in learning?

DuFour (2004) explains that teachers work together collaboratively to insure that all children learn. The focus is on *learning* rather than on teaching. Teachers work together to analyze and improve classroom practice and engage in professional dialogue with the goal of raising achievement. *Collaborative conversations* include discussing goals, strategies, materials, pacing, questions, concerns, and results. Teachers respond quickly to children who are identified as experiencing difficulty, and children are provided with the additional time and support they need as soon as they experience difficulty. Specific goals are established to improve learning, and progress is periodically evaluated.

Discussing children's progress and assessment results at regularly scheduled staff meetings provides important opportunities for teachers to share their concerns regarding problematic, challenging, or difficult behavior. Teachers should consider the time of onset of the problem(s) and the degree of frequency in which the problem occurs—is this a problem that has been ongoing, or is it a relatively new development?

The professional learning community model is effective. Teachers share ideas and strategies that they have found successful in the past with other students and new ideas from workshops, readings, or other resources, which can produce new interventions for developing skills and abilities. They support and assist each other in brainstorming interventions.

Implement Interventions

Trying new teaching strategies, giving the child additional instruction, providing a different method of teaching, and providing more opportunities for practice will help determine if there is a problem or the child just needs more time to learn. Sometimes trying new teaching methods and strategies is exactly what is needed to meet a child's unique learning style. Once teaching interventions have been identified that will aid in the child's learning, they are implemented.

Reassessment

After a reasonable period of time in which the teaching staff has implemented these new interventions and the child has had ample time to practice them, reassessing the child on those skills and abilities will demonstrate whether there has been further progress. This process is similar to the Response to Intervention (RTI) model adopted through the Individuals with Disabilities Education Act of 2004 (IDEA). The purpose of the RTI model is to catch struggling children early, provide them with assistance through appropriate instruction to maximize their learning, monitor their progress, adjust the intervention, and, ideally, prevent the need to refer them for special education.

Communicate Concerns with the Family

Concerns regarding a child's progress should always be shared with the child's family. Instead of waiting for formally scheduled family conferences, plan a meeting to communicate your concerns. Try to make the family feel respected, cared about, and not defensive about their child. Start by highlighting the child's strengths and positive characteristics. Then explain your concerns. Be prepared to provide evidence for your concerns. The more specific and concrete you can be, the more helpful the meeting will be. Bring some of the child's work samples to share, if they are relevant. Often, the work can speak for itself. Explain the following: (1) your learning objectives, (2) your concerns, (3) recent interventions that have been implemented, (4) how the child is not meeting those goals or is not making the kind of progress you might expect, and (5) what you are currently doing to address this. Ask the family if they are observing similar challenges, difficulties, or problem behaviors at home or in a variety of other settings. Engage the family in collaboration. Share with them interventions that are successful in school that also might be effective at home. Help them by giving them specific strategies and instructional activities at home that will provide consistency with what you are trying to accomplish at school. You might suggest materials they could buy for home use, or you could possibly lend them some from school. Ask the family if they have discussed their concerns with the family's pediatrician to rule out any type of health-related issues impacting the learning struggles. Ask the family if a routine vision and hearing screening has been conducted. Finally, ask the family if they will give you their permission to share this information with the child's upcoming kindergarten teacher at the end of the preschool year. This is vital information for the incoming kindergarten teachers, so they are prepared when the child enters kindergarten. In this way, kindergarten teachers will not replicate conversations and assessments that could be avoided through communication between the two schools.

NEXT STEPS: FURTHER EVALUATION AND INTERVENTION

If the family feels the child has needs that warrant further evaluation, it is the family's responsibility to contact the county or local school district to find out what services they are eligible for. The Individuals with Disabilities Education Act (IDEA) is a law ensuring services to children with disabilities throughout the country. IDEA governs how states and public agencies provide early intervention, special education, and related services to more than 6.5 million eligible infants, toddlers, children, and youth with disabilities. Infants and toddlers with disabilities (birth–2) and their families receive early intervention services under IDEA Part C. Children and youth (ages 3–21) receive special education and related services under IDEA Part B. Under IDEA, federal mandates regulate that children from birth to five years of age who are identified with disabilities will qualify for early intervention services through local Department of Special Education programs. If a child qualifies for special services, the accommodations are provided free of charge (U.S. Dept. of Education, IDEA, 2012).

Children who are three to five years old and are not yet age-eligible to attend kindergarten can receive instruction geared to their individual needs. Services provided through special day classes and small-group instruction include addressing speech, language, vision, and hearing delays; intellectual disabilities; emotional disturbances; physical, orthopedic, or other health impairments or medical disabilities; autism; and traumatic brain injury. Individualized Education Programs (IEPs) are developed for each student by a team that includes the child's parents or caregivers, private school teacher (if applicable), and the county or district's teachers, specialists, and administrators who will be working with the child (Marin County Office of Education, Special Education, Early Intervention, 2011).

CONCLUSION

Preschool teachers often have a sixth sense concerning signs of struggling in a child. When preschool teachers notice that a child is falling behind or simply not making progress in some area, discussing it with the professional learning community is an important step in determining what interventions to attempt. Having knowledge of early childhood development helps preschool teachers understand what is normal or typical behavior for a four- or five-year-old child and helps in the process of planning further assessment, discussion with the family, and possible next steps to help the child progress to his or her full potential. Determining causes and what types of outside intervention are necessary should be left to professionals through further evaluation and diagnoses.

RESOURCES

Resource 7.1	Timeline for Addressing the Needs of Struggling Children			
Action	**Date**	**Date**	**Date**	**Comments**
Assessment				
Identification of area(s) of concern				
Meeting as a professional learning community:				
1. Clarify/discuss concerns.				
2. Are there any known contributing factors?				
3. Establish goals.				
4. Brainstorm possible interventions.				
Implementation of intervention(s)				
Evaluate progress/reassessment				
Family conference				
1. Discuss concerns/ interventions.				
2. Engage in home collaboration.				
3. Possibly seek outside professional evaluation.				
Monitor progress/reassessment				
Communicate with upcoming kindergarten teacher				

Resource 7.2 Attention Deficit/Hyperactivity Disorder

Attention-deficit/hyperactivity disorder (ADHD) is a common neurobiological condition affecting 5–8 percent of school-age children with symptoms persisting into adulthood. It is characterized by developmentally inappropriate levels of inattention, impulsivity, and hyperactivity.

Although individuals with this disorder can be very successful in life, without identification and proper treatment, ADHD may have serious consequences. ADHD frequently co-occurs with other conditions such as academic or behavioral problems and emotional issues, including anxiety and learning disabilities. Children with ADHD are at risk for potentially serious problems in adolescence, including academic underachievement and school failure, problems in social relationships, family stress, depression, substance abuse, delinquency, and risk for accidental injuries. Early identification and treatment of ADHD are extremely important.

The Symptoms

Typically, ADHD symptoms arise in early childhood. Some symptoms persist into adulthood and may pose lifelong challenges. The symptom-related criteria for the three primary subtypes of ADHD are adapted from Diagnostic and Statistical Manual, fourth edition (DSM-IV). Each subtype is associated with different symptoms and is summarized below. Some of the symptoms that a preschool-age child might demonstrate include the following:

ADHD—Primarily Inattentive Type:

- Has difficulty sustaining attention
- Does not appear to listen
- Struggles to follow through on instructions
- Has difficulty with organization
- Avoids or dislikes tasks requiring sustained mental effort
- Loses things
- Is easily distracted
- Is forgetful in daily activities

ADHD—Primarily Hyperactive/Impulsive Type:

- Fidgets with hands or feet or squirms in chair
- Has difficulty remaining seated
- Runs around or climbs excessively
- Has difficulty engaging in activities quietly
- Acts as if driven by a motor
- Talks excessively
- Blurts out answers before questions have been completed
- Has difficulty waiting or taking turns
- Interrupts or intrudes upon others

ADHD—Combined Type:

- Meets both inattentive and hyperactive/impulsive criteria

(Continued)

(Continued)

> Several types of professionals can diagnose ADHD, including clinical psychologists, clinical social workers, nurse practitioners, neurologists, psychiatrists, and pediatricians. A medical exam by a pediatrician is important and should include a thorough physical examination, including assessment of hearing and vision, to rule out other medical problems that may be causing symptoms similar to ADHD.

Source: Children and Adults with Attention-Deficit/Hyperactivity Disorder (CHADD), 2012. Adapted with permission.

PROFESSIONAL DEVELOPMENT DISCUSSION GUIDE

1. Deepen Your Thinking:
   a. Choose one of these inquiry topics for group discussion:
      i. Think of a child in your program whom you have some concerns about. Try to articulate exactly what you have been observing that gives you cause for concern. Discuss your thoughts with your professional learning community.
      ii. What if a family initiates a conversation with you about certain concerns they have about their child? What steps would you take?

WHERE CAN I LEARN MORE?

Autism Information Page: National Institute of Neurological Disorders and Stroke
http://www.ninds.nih.gov/disorders/autism/autism.htm

Children and Adults with Attention Deficit/Hyperactivity Disorder (CHADD)
http://www.chadd.org

Council for Exceptional Children (CEC) http://www.cec.sped.org.

Dyslexia Information Page: National Institute of Neurological Disorders and Stroke
http://www.ninds.nih.gov/disorders/dyslexia/dyslexia.htm

Harvard Education Letter, Harvard Graduate School of Education
http://www.hepg.org/main/hel/Index.html

LD Online (website on Learning Disabilities and ADHD)
http://www.ldonline.org/index.php

Marin County Office of Education, Special Education, California Early Start Program
http://jade.marinschools.org/Student-Programs/Special-Education/Pages/Early
-Start.aspx

Marin County Office of Education, Special Education, Early Intervention http://jade
.marinschools.org/Student-Programs/Special-Education/Pages/Early-Intervention
.aspx

National Center for Early Development and Learning (NCEDL)
http://www.fpg.unc.edu/~ncedl/index.cfm

National Institute for Early Education Research (NIEER) http://www.nieer.org.

National Institute of Child Health and Human Development (NICHD)
http://www.nichd.nih.gov

National Institute of Mental Health (NIMH) http://www.nimh.nih.gov

National Resource Center on ADHD http://www.help4adhd.org/

U.S. Department of Education, Individuals with Disabilities Act (IDEA)
http://idea.ed.gov/

8 Partnering With Families

The Family's Role in Kindergarten Readiness

Families are an important component in making sure the child is ready for school. Informing families about the multidimensional framework of kindergarten readiness helps them proactively partner with you in the process of preparing their children for kindergarten. Help families understand that kindergarten readiness is not one attribute or quality but the interrelationship of the domains of early learning and development—physical well-being and motor development, social development, emotional development, approaches toward learning, language and communication development, emerging literacy development, and cognitive development and general knowledge. Explain to families that kindergarten readiness comprises many components—the characteristics, skills, and abilities of the individual child; the quality of the preschool experience; the transition to kindergarten; *and* the characteristics of the child's family. When families understand that early childhood experiences in all these areas of learning and development are intricately linked to later school success and that they are all interrelated, then they will be more likely to knowledgeably and actively participate in the process of preparing their children for kindergarten. A family-oriented explanation of each domain of early learning and development with suggestions for activities to strengthen the child's skills and abilities in each area is provided in Resource 8.1.

FREQUENTLY ASKED QUESTIONS BY FAMILIES OF PRESCHOOL-AGE CHILDREN

How Will I Know If My Child Is Ready for Kindergarten?

The more families understand about the complexity of kindergarten readiness, the more they will realize that being certain their child is ready for kindergarten may be difficult to determine! They are not alone. There is no easy answer! All states have age requirements for entering kindergartners, so this is the first place to start—is the child age-eligible for kindergarten? Many families choose to "redshirt" their children, holding them back another year before enrolling them in kindergarten in the hopes they will be *more* ready because they will be older and will have had more time to get ready. Sometimes other factors come into play when families decide whether to send their children to kindergarten. These include

- Financial responsibilities and commitments
  - the cost of preschool or day care
  - parents' needing to go back to work
- Ages, grades, schools, and schedules of the child's siblings

Most frequently, however, families are concerned that their child may not demonstrate characteristics that they think are necessary for kindergarten success. Frequently this includes the child's ability to read, write, and count. But, as has been discussed in Chapter 3, kindergarten teachers emphasize the importance of social and emotional readiness over academic readiness.

The Family Questionnaire (Resource 8.2) asks the family to answer several questions about their child. These questions address skills and characteristics in all of the domains and help make the decision less abstract. You can refer to these questions when discussing a family's concern regarding their child's readiness.

It is also helpful for families to be aware of the kinds of information their new kindergarten may be seeking about their incoming students. Although many schools do not solicit information about their incoming students from their feeder preschools, the questions included in the Preschool Faculty Questionnaire in Chapter 9 (Resource 9.2) are indicative of the kinds of abilities, characteristics, and skills typical of incoming kindergartners that the kindergarten teachers will want to know about. Most important, they involve a balance of social, emotional, behavioral, and academic abilities.

Remember that *all* children show a wide range of strengths and abilities in each domain, and *no* child will be uniformly strong in all areas. There are not one, two, or three things a child *has* to know or be able to do. *No* child will be turned away from kindergarten if he or she is age-eligible, no matter how *ready* or not he or she is. Remind the family that it is the *school's* responsibility to be ready for *all* entering kindergartners. Kindergarten readiness is a balancing act. A family wants to feel that its child has sufficient strengths *overall* to be successful in kindergarten.

What Will My Child Be Expected to Learn and Be Able to Do During the Kindergarten Year?

While most private schools have more latitude in determining their curricula for instruction and determining what children need to know and be able to do by the end of kindergarten, public kindergartens are accountable for teaching children according to their individual kindergarten State Content Standards and the kindergarten Common Core Standards in English/ Language Arts and Mathematics. For a discussion and list of the Common Core Content Standards, see Chapter 4 and Resources 4.5 and 4.6.

How Can We, as a Family, Help Prepare Our Child for Kindergarten?

Families can contribute more than they may realize to their child's readiness for kindergarten. Besides having their children attend a high-quality preschool or other developmentally appropriate early learning environment, providing a nurturing home environment that supports learning is critical. This seemingly simple fact is especially troublesome, however, for the increasing number of families that have limited resources. Children who come from a positive literacy environment, who possess a positive approach toward learning, and who enjoy very good or excellent health perform better academically than children who do not have these advantages, and these benefits persist into later grades (Denton & West, 2002; Princiotta, Flanagan, & Germino Hausken, 2006; Walston, Rathbun, & Germino Hausken, 2008). Children who begin kindergarten with certain resources are at a developmental advantage. The advantages, as well as the disadvantages, with which children begin school are also sustainable over time.

In general, positive attitudes toward learning; exposure to, exploration of, and engagement in the outside world; language experiences; social interactions; and exposure to print all help to nurture the young child's development and readiness for school. Resource 8.1 provides activities that families can engage in to promote their child's growth in all domains of early learning and development. Most important, encourage families to read to and with their children! Libraries are excellent resources for children's books and programs at no cost to families.

What Can We Do to Ensure the Kindergarten Experience Is a Positive One for Our Child?

It is widely recognized that parental involvement in a child's education generally benefits the child's learning and overall school success. The more that the child's school (and in particular, the kindergarten classroom) invites families to be an integral part of the classroom learning environment, the greater the family-school partnership will be. There are many ways for families to be actively involved in the classroom *if* the kindergarten program establishes these opportunities *and* accommodates families' busy schedules. These include allowing parents to volunteer in the classroom by leading learning centers; helping with technology, art, cooking, or science projects; helping with class or school events; joining in field trips; and encouraging parents to attend teacher-family conferences. Open and frequent communication with the teacher is also important to staying informed and maintaining a positive and supportive relationship.

How Do We Know If the Kindergarten We Choose Is the Right Fit for Our Child?

Many families have the option of choosing a private or charter school for their child to attend instead of their local public kindergarten. This choice requires conscientious effort and investigation to ensure that not only the kindergarten class but the overall school is indeed a good match for their child. There are many factors that go into this decision. Whether families are exploring options for private school or they just want to know more about their public school, they need to consider the varied components. Resource 8.3 provides a list of factors to consider.

CONCLUSION

The family plays a vital part in a child's readiness for and transition to kindergarten. Families who understand the complexity of kindergarten readiness, are informed about their child's progress in preschool, understand what they can do in the home environment to help prepare their child for kindergarten, and have established a communicative and collaborative partnership with their preschool and kindergarten will most likely contribute positively to their child's early start in school.

Resource 8.1 Family Activities in All Domains of Early Learning and Development

Physical Well-Being and Motor Development

This domain encompasses the characteristics, skills, and abilities of a child's physical health and overall well-being; self-help skills; fitness; and gross motor, fine motor, sensorimotor, and graphomotor abilities. Healthy children enjoy a freedom that allows them to focus on or actively engage in experiences crucial to the learning process. Encourage developing abilities in the following areas:

- Gross Motor
  o Running, jumping, hopping, skipping, climbing, kicking, throwing, catching
- Fine Motor
  o Manipulating small objects: Legos, small blocks and puzzles, buttons, clothes pins, paintbrushes, sewing cards, hole punch, glue stick, scissors
- Sensorimotor
  o Playing in water (pouring; playing with turkey basters, brushes, and spray bottles); playing in sand (digging and scooping); playing with finger paint, clay
- Graphomotor
  o Proper pencil grip and writing posture
  o Use of crayons, chalk, colored markers, and pencils
  o Trace and copy shapes, numbers, and letters

(Continued)

(Continued)

- o Color within lines
- o Draw a person

- Self-Help Skills

  - o Dressing, feeding, attending to bathroom needs
  - o Cleaning up
  - o Adjusting to transitions and routines
  - o Completing an activity independently

- Overall Health

  - o Sufficient sleep and nutrition
  - o Stamina
  - o Mental alertness

Social Development

This domain encompasses the characteristics, skills, and abilities that enable children to have secure and successful interactions and relationships with others, including peers, teachers, and other adults. Help children develop positive relationships with others by helping them

- respect the right of others and keep to their own space.
- form and sustain new friendships.
- develop sensitivity to other children's feelings.
- respect differences and perspectives of others.
- cooperate and play with other children.
- resolve conflict nonaggressively and by using compromising strategies.
- take turns and share.

Emotional Development

This domain encompasses the characteristics, skills, and abilities that enable children to have positive feelings about themselves and demonstrate self-control in the classroom setting. Help children strengthen their self-concept, self-awareness, and self-regulation of emotions and behavior by encouraging them to

- discuss their own feelings as well as those of others (i.e., fear, anger, grief, frustration).
- express and articulate feelings and emotions.
- understand the impact of their behavior.
- understand consequences of their behavior.
- demonstrate self-control.
- self-regulate emotions and behavior.
- feel self-confidence and pride in their work.

Approaches Toward Learning

This domain encompasses the inclinations, dispositions, and styles reflective of the ways children become engaged in learning and approach learning tasks. Help children's involvement in learning by encouraging them to

- accept new challenges willingly.
- persevere with difficult tasks.
- maintain effort and mental endurance.
- approach new activities with enthusiasm, and eagerness, and curiosity.
- demonstrate imagination and invention.
- ask questions.
- focus on and attend to an activity or task for 10 minutes or more.
- seek help when needed.
- share a positive orientation toward school.
- positively manage transitions and separations.

Language and Communication Development

This domain encompasses the characteristics, skills, and abilities enabling children to express themselves and communicate with others. Help children acquire greater abilities in receptive (listening) and expressive (speaking) language and communication skills by encouraging them to

- listen to, repeat, and follow two-step directions.
- ask and answer questions.
- express ideas and thoughts clearly in their primary language.
- communicate needs, wants, and thoughts clearly in English.
- listen attentively to a story for 10 or more minutes.
- engage in conversations.
- sing songs.
- read books with others.
- tell stories with others.
- build word meaning and new vocabulary.

Emerging Literacy

This domain encompasses skills and abilities having to do with the acquisition of phonemic awareness and emergent reading skills and communication in written form. Help strengthen these skills by surrounding the child with print and writing tools. Help the child understand that pictures and words convey meaning and give us knowledge about the world. Encourage the child in the following areas:

- Emergent Reading

  o Look at books of all kinds independently: picture, story, poems, concepts, nonfiction, and "how-to."
  o Develop alphabetic and phonemic awareness.

    - Recognize and identify upper- and lowercase letters.
    - Identify letter sounds.
    - Identify and produce rhyming words.

  o Develop book awareness and demonstrate an understanding of concepts of print.
  o Recognize environmental print (i.e., *stop, exit, open*).

(Continued)

(Continued)

- o Develop story sense.
    - Retell the story.
    - Sequence events in the story.
- o Build comprehension.
    - Answer questions about the story, the setting, the characters, the problem or main idea
- Emergent Writing
    - o Draw pictures and dictate stories.
    - o Write scribbles, letters, sounds, words, and/or sentences.
    - o Write first name.

As a parent, you can also

- ask questions, speak, and listen to your child.
- share your love of reading with your family.
- model reading and writing both inside and outside the home.

Cognitive Development and General Knowledge

This domain encompasses the knowledge base a child has and the child's ability to construct, understand, acquire, and represent the world cognitively within three types of knowledge—physical, logico-mathematical, and social-conventional. Through play, children explore, discover, question, converse, and learn about the world. Encourage children in the following areas:

- Physical Knowledge
    - o Observing, asking questions, and solving problems
    - o Gaining exposure to, learning, and exploring the natural world through their environment
    - o Identifying shapes and colors
    - o Drawing pictures to represent events, people, places, and things
    - o Relating cause to effect
    - o Making predictions
    - o Distinguishing real from pretend
    - o Comparing and contrasting
        - Recognizing relationships, similarities, and differences among objects
    - o Problem solving
- Social Knowledge
    - o Understanding the purpose of rules
    - o Understanding social-conventional norms
    - o Understanding the difference between right and wrong behavior in specific situations
    - o Understanding adult roles and demonstrating compliance with teachers and authority figures
- Logico-mathematical knowledge
    - o Sequencing events
    - o Making, copying, and extending patterns

o Sorting, classifying, and ordering objects
o Numeracy
  • Counting objects
  • Recognizing and writing numbers

Resource 8.2   Family Questionnaire: Is My Child Ready for Kindergarten?

Have the family answer these questions about their child:

- Does my child take care of his or her personal needs such as cleaning up after himself or herself, attending to his or her bathroom needs, finding his or her belongings, and putting things away?
- Does my child generally approach new activities and new situations with curiosity and enthusiasm?
- Can my child identify colors and shapes?
- Does my child express his or her emotions and feelings to others?
- Does my child form new friendships easily?
- Does my child usually pay attention to a story or attend to an activity for 10 minutes or more?
- Does my child handle difficult or challenging tasks without getting frustrated?
- Does my child concentrate and persist in completing a task or activity?
- Can my child write some of the letters of the alphabet?
- Does my child remember and follow directions without having them repeated?
- Does my child know and understand that there are consequences for his or her behavior?
- Does my child demonstrate self-control when he or she does not get his or her way?
- Can my child rhyme?
- Does my child take turns and share with other children easily?
- Can my child count, recognize, and write numbers to 10?
- Does my child work out problems or conflicts with other children independently and nonaggressively?
- Does my child know how to read?
- Can my child draw a picture of a person and use scissors, glue sticks, and markers?
- Does my child like to build with Legos and blocks?
- Does my child separate from me without anxiety?
- Does my child communicate his or her needs, wants, and thoughts clearly in English? In our primary language?
- Can my child write letters, words, and numbers?
- Does my child respect the rights of others?
- Can my child throw, catch, and kick balls; run; hop; jump; skip; and climb?
- Does my child cooperate and play with other children?
- Does my child use age-appropriate vocabulary?
- Does my child know some of the letters and sounds of the alphabet?
- Does my child enjoy looking at books independently?
- Does my child demonstrate compliance with us (parents), teachers, and other authority figures?
- Can my child hold a pencil with the proper grip?
- Can my child retell a familiar story?
- Can my child write his or her name?

Resource 8.3   What to Consider When Choosing a Kindergarten

The Overall School

1. Location (proximity to home/work)

2. Grades levels in available in the school (K–5, K–8, etc.)

3. Single-gender or coed

4. Religious or other affiliation/orientation

5. Is this kindergarten a feeder school for a certain middle or high school? (Are the students guided to a specific middle or high school after leaving this school?)

6. Family involvement, participation, expectations, and communication

7. Financial commitment

8. Length of school day (hours of operation) and school-year schedule

9. Extended day care programs/afterschool clubs and sports

10. Mission statement/educational philosophy

11. Student enrollment size

12. Diversity of children and staff

13. Student/teacher ratio

14. Average class size

15. Student support services and resources (school psychologist, learning specialist, reading specialist)

16. Instructional methodology and teaching style in kindergarten and beyond (child-directed, problem-based, inquiry, teacher-directed)

17. Technology, music, P.E., art, foreign languages, drama, library

18. Measures of safety, supervision, emergency information and plans

19. Faculty qualifications and longevity

The Kindergarten Classroom

1. Number of kindergarten classrooms

2. Curriculum, learning activities, and materials

3. Schedule/structure of the day

4. Physical environment: outside space (types of equipment and play opportunities)

5. Physical environment: inside space (range and type of classroom materials, equipment, and activities)

By visiting the kindergarten classroom on a typical school day, observe the following:

- Interactions among children
- Interactions between teachers and children (caring, sharing, helping, problem solving, negotiating, resolving conflict, cooperating, talking, questioning, disciplining)

- Classroom areas and spaces
- Classroom groupings (individual/small/large group activities)
- Instruction, activities, or opportunities for language and literacy development (reading and writing)

Finally, ask yourself the following questions:

- Is this school the right fit for my child?
- Is this school the right fit for me?
- Would this be the right fit for my child's sibling(s)?
- Do the goals/values/philosophy of the school match ours at home? Will there be consistency?
- Will my child's strengths, challenges, interests, and needs be met, addressed, and nurtured?
- Will my child be happy here for up to ____ years?

PROFESSIONAL DEVELOPMENT DISCUSSION GUIDE

1. Deepen Your Thinking:

   a. Choose one or more of these individual inquiry topics for group discussion

      1. What will I tell a family if they ask me if I think their child is ready for kindergarten?
      2. What will I tell a family they might do at home to help prepare their child for kindergarten?

WHERE CAN I LEARN MORE?

California Association for the Education of Young Children http://www.caeyc.org

Kindergarten Common Core Content Standards in English/Language Arts http://www.corestandards.org/the-standards/english-language-arts-standards

Kindergarten Common Core Content Standards in Mathematics http://www.corestandards.org/the-standards/mathematics

International Reading Association http://www.reading.org

National Association for the Education of Young Children http://www.naeyc.org

National Institute for Early Educational Research http://www.nieer.org

Your local library

The Transition to Kindergarten

Alignment and Transition

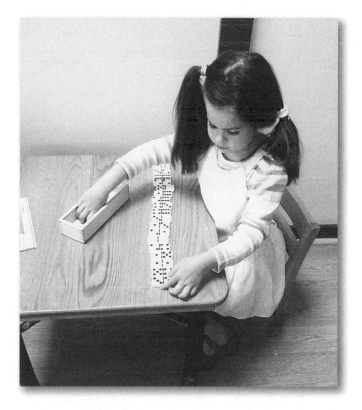

The transition between preschool and kindergarten is an exciting time, but it is also one that presents a number of challenges for many children. A successful transition depends on many factors to ensure the child experiences a smooth and successful adjustment to kindergarten. Smooth transitions involve what has been called *purposeful coordination* between the various contexts involved: the child, the family, the preschool, the home, the kindergarten classroom, and the kindergarten and preschool teachers prior to the start of kindergarten (Early, Pianta, Taylor, & Cox, 2001). Not only do smooth transitions ultimately aid in children's readiness for kindergarten, but they also provide children with positive experiences at the start of school that consequently support children's early school success.

Transition practices are the use of specific activities that facilitate the continuity and foster the interrelationship among the various contexts. Transition practices have been shown to facilitate quicker social and emotional adjustment to kindergarten, which evidence suggests enables children to take better advantage of learning opportunities in the classroom and is also a precursor and predictor of later school success (Kagan, Carroll, Comer, & Scott-Little, 2006; Rimm-Kaufman, Pianta, & Cox, 2000). Since the goals, demands, and expectations of kindergarten are different from those of preschool and because of children's diverse experiences preceding kindergarten, some children are more successful than others in meeting the new demands of kindergarten. Studies indicate that children may even be at greater risk for both school failure and social adjustment problems when they experience an ineffective transition between preschool and kindergarten (LoCasale-Crouch, Mashburn, Downer, & Pianta, 2008).

Unfortunately, transition practices have been identified as an underutilized means of preparing children for the adjustment to kindergarten. In the National Center for Early Development and Learning's (NCEDL) *Multi-State Prekindergarten Study* during the 2001–2002 school year, it was found that transition practices that involve kindergarten teachers' individualized communication with children, families, and schools before the start of kindergarten, including visits from kindergarten teachers to preschool classrooms, were the least frequently used. The most frequently reported transition practices are those that occur *after* children begin kindergarten, described as "too little, too late, and too impersonal" (LoCasale-Crouch et al., 2008, p. 126).

Kindergarten teachers have indicated that many children demonstrate different problems as they enter kindergarten. One of the questions in the NCEDL's *Transition Practices Survey* (Rimm-Kaufman et al., 2000) asked teachers what kinds of problems children in a typical class experienced when they entered kindergarten. Kindergarten teachers listed the following twelve problems: (1) lack of academic skills; (2) difficulty following directions; (3) difficulty working as part of a group; (4) problems with social skills, such as getting along with other children; (5) difficulty working independently; (6) difficulty communicating/language problems; (7) lack of any formal preschool experience; (8) highly academic preschool experience; (9) nonacademic preschool experience; (10) disorganized home environments; (11) immaturity; and (12) other. Findings indicated that over one-third of the teachers reported that "about half the class or more" entered kindergarten with "difficulty following directions," "lack of academic skills," "disorganized home environment," and "difficulty working independently." Forty-six percent of the teachers reported that "about half the class or more" had "difficulty following directions," whereas only 14 percent of the teachers reported that "about half the class or more" had "difficulty communicating/language problems" (Rimm-Kaufman et al., 2000).

Nine common transition practices identified by the NCEDL's *Transition Practices Survey* included (1) preschool children's visits to kindergarten classes, (2) preschool teachers' visits to kindergarten classes, (3) kindergarten teachers' visits to preschool, (4) spring orientation meetings for preschool children, (5) spring orientation meetings for preschool children's parents, (6) schoolwide elementary school activities for preschool children, (7) individual meetings between preschool teachers and preschool children's parents about kindergarten, (8) preschools sharing written records about children's preschool experience with the elementary school, and (9) communication between preschool teachers and kindergarten teachers regarding curriculum and/or specific children. It was found that, although *some* form of transition practice was universal, the most frequently reported practice (employed by 95 percent of the 3,595 respondents) was kindergarten teachers talking with the child's parents once school began (Pianta, Cox, Taylor, & Early, 1999).

Overall, transition practices in preschool are positively associated with children's readiness and adjustment to kindergarten. In fact, the positive influence of transition practices was found to be stronger for children who experienced social and economic risk. Outreach efforts between kindergarten and preschool continue to be an underutilized and overlooked practice that has important implications for children's adjustment and readiness to kindergarten (LoCasale-Crouch et al., 2008).

An essential element of transition is the intentional and focused emphasis on the coordination of standards, curriculum, and assessments, in which the child's development is the key focus or goal. Efforts to provide consistency and continuity across these contexts are often referred to as *alignment. Vertical alignment*—consistency and continuity between preschool's curriculum and kindergarten's content standards—has important implications for the degree to which children experience consistency and continuity as they transition from the preschool to kindergarten setting (Kagan et al., 2006). Closely aligned early learning standards and kindergarten standards can promote consistency and continuity for children as they transition from preschool into kindergarten.

Successful transition requires not only that children demonstrate readiness for school but that *schools* be ready to adapt to the diverse and changing needs of *all* young children. The National Education Goals Panel's (NEGP) focus on "ready schools" attempted to smooth the transition between home and school, striving for continuity between early education programs and elementary schools, recognizing the many interrelated resources that support children's success. The NEGP claimed that it is the responsibility of schools to provide continuity and a smooth transition between kindergarten and home, early care, and early education; to educate children effectively; and to promote school success once children begin school (Shore, 1998).

The transition to kindergarten must be conceptualized not in terms of the individual child's readiness abilities, skills, and characteristics but in the combined efforts and collaboration among schools, teachers, and families in ways that support children's adjustment to kindergarten. These positive early links optimize a child's ability to start school successfully, support the child's adjustment into kindergarten, and impact subsequent school success. The lack of kindergarten teachers' outreach attempts has been found to be the trend, even though these transitional practices are beneficial for both kindergarten teachers and incoming kindergarten students. It is imperative that schools provide opportunities, time, and resources to encourage transitional and alignment practices to kindergarten.

In order to aid in the development of stronger transition practices aimed at preparing children for the adjustment to kindergarten through greater collaboration, communication, and consistency between preschools, families, and kindergarten, the nine transition practices identified by Pianta et al. (1999) have been expanded by the author to thirteen transition practices based on her use of current transitional practices in one Northern California county. These thirteen practices provide a comprehensive transitional process spanning several months, from the spring until the fall. Underlying these practices is the belief that a strong partnership between families and schools will benefit children's experiences at school. Communication, inclusion, collaboration, and participation are key. These suggested 13 transition practices are described below, in the order in which they would occur in the academic year. A suggested timeline is provided in Resource 9.1. Although it would be optimal to implement all of the 13 practices within the year, starting with any of them and building onto them each year is a great start!

Please note: There may be several preschools in one area that feed into one or more public schools. Although it might be difficult to involve *all* the preschools that feed into the kindergarten classrooms, every attempt to collaborate between local preschools and those kindergarten teachers who will be receiving the incoming students is ideal. These transition practices apply to private kindergarten classes as well.

TRANSITION PRACTICES

1. Meeting and exchanging information between preschool teachers and kindergarten teachers

This initial meeting between preschool teachers and kindergarten teachers serving children in the same district is an informal and important way to meet each other. The purpose of this meeting is to share information and discuss each other's programs, curriculum, goals, and expectations. Open communication, articulation of ideas, and exchanges of information and experiences with children in the classroom setting are encouraged. This is the start of collaboration and alignment between preschool and kindergarten.

2. Preschool classroom and kindergarten classroom teacher observation exchange

Preschool teachers observe in the kindergarten classrooms (in schools where most of their students will be attending), and kindergarten teachers observe in some of the preschool classrooms (where many of the entering kindergartners will have attended) to learn more about each other's programs. The observations in each other's classroom learning environments provide a valuable opportunity to see children in action as they play, interact with other children and adults, and respond to and approach specific learning activities. It gives teachers a realistic picture of what occurs in these different and less-familiar learning environments.

3. Family informational meeting: kindergarten readiness

Families know very little about kindergarten readiness, so it is our responsibility to educate them. With greater knowledge of the components of kindergarten readiness and specific suggestions for what families can do at home to help their children prepare for kindergarten, the school-family partnership will be strengthened, and families will feel more knowledgeable about how they can optimally prepare their children for the newly approaching kindergarten expectations and curriculum. Schedule a presentation on the topic of kindergarten readiness specifically geared to families of preschoolers. Invite the families of all the preschoolers to attend this informal meeting, given by a professional in the field, to learn more about readiness and what families can do at home to help prepare their children for kindergarten. (See Chapter 8 for more on the topic.) This informative meeting helps settle anxieties about what families believe their children have to know and be able to do before the start of kindergarten and gives them a sense of empowerment as they learn what they can do to contribute to and facilitate this process.

4. Preschool conference: preschool teachers and families of preschoolers

The spring conference between the preschool director and/or head teacher and the preschooler's family is an important juncture in the transition process. This conference provides an appropriate time for the preschool staff to inform the family about the child's abilities, skills, behavior, social skills, and growth during the year. Important points can include discussing the child's strengths and challenges in areas that pertain to kindergarten readiness. This meeting provides a safe and confidential setting in which the preschool faculty can listen to any concerns or questions the family has regarding their child's readiness for kindergarten. Although these conferences are not mandatory, all families should be encouraged to attend, and appointments should be scheduled to maximize families' participation.

5. Kindergarten visit

Families applying to private schools have the opportunity to visit those schools. However, families with children entering the public school's kindergarten often do not get the opportunity to look beyond the doors of their child's new kindergarten classroom. To help ease the anxiety many families feel about their children entering a new school setting, the elementary school can schedule a number of visitations open to families of incoming kindergarten students to allow them to briefly visit the kindergarten classrooms during the school day. The tour leaders should be parent volunteers of current elementary school students or teachers from that school. A short question-and-answer period with the elementary school's administrator should follow, so incoming families can learn more about the new school and the kindergarten program. This visitation serves to welcome new families into the school community. It also provides a way for incoming families to meet each other, particularly since families from different preschools and community settings will attend this visitation.

6. Preschool questionnaire

The information the administrator and kindergarten team receives about the incoming kindergarten students is extremely useful in creating balanced classrooms for the start of school. The information helps prepare kindergarten teachers for their incoming classes of kindergarten students. A questionnaire designed to be completed by the preschool director or head teacher for each preschooler entering kindergarten in the fall helps supply important information about each student's skills, abilities, and characteristics as they pertain to the classroom environment. A sample preschool questionnaire is provided (Resource 9.2).

7. Family survey

This survey asks families to answer questions about their children's skills, abilities, and characteristics from the family's unique perspective. It provides additional valuable information for the kindergarten team about the family's perception of the child and how the child interacts, plays, and behaves in the home environment. A sample letter of introduction and family survey are provided (Resources 9.3 and 9.4).

8. *Sneak peek* visit in a kindergarten classroom

Allowing entering kindergartners the opportunity to take a *sneak peek* into the new world of kindergarten gives them an unequivocal preview of what they will experience in the new school year. All families of children registered to enter kindergarten in the fall are invited to this special event. Kindergarten teachers open their classrooms after school and have small groups of children and their families spend 30–45 minutes in the classroom. The kindergartners-to-be, in the comforting presence of their families, can explore many of the materials and activities in the classroom. New families get a taste of what a kindergarten classroom is like, too. At the same time, the kindergarten teachers, administrator, and support staff, can observe the children at play. Administering an informal and innocuous assessment, such as having children draw a self-portrait and write their name, can also provide further information about the incoming students.

9. Kindergarten teacher-generated class list

With the help of a compilation of all the information the school has received from the kindergarten registration forms, the family survey, the preschool questionnaire, and the sneak peek, the administrator works with the kindergarten team to create the most *balanced* classrooms possible for the fall. *Balanced* classrooms are those that have a heterogeneous mix of children in each classroom. This mix is composed of children from different preschools, socioeconomic backgrounds, skills, abilities, and ethnicities. Each class is balanced in terms of gender and is inclusive of children with recognized challenges and special needs and those who are English language learners.

10. Summer kindergarten readiness program

The purpose of a summer kindergarten readiness program is to prepare children for the kind of classroom learning environment that they will encounter when they enter kindergarten. Ideally, this program has the following characteristics:

- The program is held in a kindergarten classroom in the school in which the child is enrolled. In the event that space cannot be allocated for this purpose, the program can be held in another location that is licensed for young children (i.e., parks and recreation classroom or religious school classroom).
- The program is taught by a certificated kindergarten teacher currently teaching in that school who is familiar with the school and the kindergarten program or from a similar kindergarten program.
- The goal of this one-week, half-day program is to address developmental skills and abilities in all areas of early learning and development: physical (gross motor, fine motor, and graphomotor), emotional, social, early literacy, communication, language, and cognitive development.
- All entering kindergartners from the community are welcome to enroll, regardless of what school they will be attending for kindergarten. (This is because very few schools have this kind of program at all.) A sample summer kindergarten readiness program informational letter is provided (Resource 9.5).

11. Kindergarten orientation

The day before school begins, kindergartners have the opportunity to visit their assigned kindergarten classroom and meet their teacher and fellow classmates. This orientation helps ease the new kindergartner into the school day routine. The kindergarten teacher will plan introductions and some time to read, play, and answer children's questions about kindergarten. In general, this hourlong orientation helps children get excited about the first day of school, reduces the anxiety the children may be feeling about being left by themselves for the first entire day of school, and allows the children to get accustomed to their new classroom. An orientation letter to families informs families of things they need to know right away for the first few days of school. Having families fill out a short family questionnaire to be returned the next day (Resource 9.6) also provides the kindergarten teacher with necessary logistical and personal information.

12. School begins: building classroom community, communication, family involvement, and partnerships

Beginning the first day of school, kindergarten teachers will want to ensure that their new students are adjusting to the new routines, schedules, expectations, and demands of kindergarten and that all the students' families feel welcomed to the new classroom community. Building a classroom community through rapport, communication, respect, and collaboration sets the tone for positive relationships and partnerships between the teacher and families throughout the kindergarten year. Invite families to become actively involved in their children's education during the kindergarten year through volunteer opportunities in the classroom and schoolwide events. Inform them of all upcoming activities—in particular, Back to School Night or Welcome to Kindergarten Night, at which time they will learn more about the kindergarten program for the year.

13. Kindergarten conference: kindergarten teacher and families of kindergartners

The first conference between the kindergarten teacher and the student's family early in the fall provides an excellent opportunity for them to formally meet each other and share information about the child. The teacher might want to open the dialogue by asking the question "How is your child adjusting to kindergarten?" The teacher will learn more about the student through the family's perspective, and families will learn more about their child's abilities, skills, and social skills in the new classroom. The teacher can inform the family of the child's progress and adjustment in the classroom during the first month of school, and the family can ask questions or express their own concerns. Important points would include discussing the child's strengths and challenges in areas the teacher/and/or the family want to focus on. Although these conferences are not mandatory, all families should be encouraged to attend, and appointments should be scheduled to accommodate families' schedules in order to maximize their participation.

CONCLUSION

These 13 transition practices gradually scaffold and support the move from home and preschool to kindergarten. They are important components of school readiness and the child's subsequent success in kindergarten. Although the trend in the past has been that these transition practices are underutilized by both preschool teachers and kindergarten teachers, it is hoped that the trend will change so that transition practices become more frequently utilized by all preschools and kindergartens to support the successful transition from preschool to kindergarten. This requires not only ensuring that children have readiness competencies but also examining the expectations of the schools that they will attend.

Resource 9.1 Transition Practices Timeline

	Date	Practice	Purpose
1	Late March	Meeting between preschool teachers and kindergarten teachers	Preschool teachers and kindergarten teachers meet informally for open communication, articulation of ideas, and exchanges of information and experiences.
2	Early April	Preschool classroom and kindergarten classroom observation exchange	Preschool teachers observe in the kindergarten classroom and kindergarten teachers observe in the preschool classroom to learn more about each other's programs and see students in action.
3	Mid-April	Family informational meeting: kindergarten readiness	Families of preschoolers are invited to learn more about kindergarten readiness and what they can do to help their children.
4	Early May	Preschool conference	Each preschool teacher meets with each preschooler's family to discuss the preschooler's progress and readiness for kindergarten.
5	Early May	Kindergarten visit	Incoming families visit the kindergarten classrooms to learn more about the kindergarten program.
6	Mid-May	Preschool questionnaire	These questionnaires, completed by preschool staff, provide information to the kindergarten teachers about each student's abilities and skills in preschool.
7	Mid-May	Family survey	The family of each incoming kindergartner answers questions about their child's abilities, skills, and behavior at home to inform teachers of each child's strengths and challenges.
8	Early June	*Sneak peek* visit in a kindergarten classroom	Incoming kindergartners are allowed to see for themselves what the kindergarten classroom is like, and kindergarten teachers and staff are given an opportunity to observe the children.
9	Mid-June	Kindergarten teachers generate class lists	The elementary administrator and kindergarten team create kindergarten class lists to promote balanced classes.
10	Mid- to late August	Summer kindergarten readiness program	This optional weeklong readiness program is designed to prepare entering kindergartners for school and is modeled after a typical kindergarten learning environment.
11	Day before school officially begins	Kindergarten orientation	Kindergarten orientation helps children get excited about the first day of school and reduces the anxiety they may be feeling.
12	First or second week of school	School begins: building classroom community, communication, family involvement, and partnerships	The kindergarten teacher welcomes families into the classroom community and invites them to participate in the school.
13	Fourth week of school	Kindergarten conferences	The kindergarten teacher meets with kindergartner's family to discuss child's adjustment to kindergarten.

Resource 9.2 Preschool Faculty Questionnaire for Entering Kindergartners

---

To families: Please complete the top part of this form and give it to your child's current preschool teacher with the attached preaddressed envelope. Remember to add a postage stamp. Thank you!

Child's name: _____

Birth date: _____

Preschool name: _____

Preschool phone number: _____

Dear Preschool Teachers,

In order to create balanced Kindergarten classes at _____ School and to give us insight into each entering kindergartner's readiness, we are requesting that you complete the following checklist for this child. This information is extremely helpful and strictly *confidential!* Please be as honest, candid, and objective as possible. Please place this form in the attached envelope and mail to: _____ School, _____ (address) _____ (by May _____, if possible).

Please call _____ School with any questions _____ (phone number).

Check the selection that most describes this child.

Behavioral/Social/Emotional Readiness Abilities

Usually plays: alone _____ with others _____ or both _____

Cooperates with and shares with others: most of the time _____ sometimes _____ rarely _____

Follows classroom routines: most of the time _____ sometimes _____ rarely _____

Asks teachers for help: most of the time _____ sometimes _____ rarely _____

Demonstrates self-control: most of the time _____ sometimes _____ rarely _____

Demonstrates independence: most of the time _____ sometimes _____ rarely _____

Requires teacher supervision/attention: often _____ frequently _____ rarely _____

Takes care of his/her personal needs: most of the time _____ sometimes _____ rarely _____

(Continued)

(Continued)

Expresses and explains ideas/feelings/thoughts: frequently _____ sometimes _____ rarely _____

Forms new friendships easily: most of the time _____ sometimes _____ rarely _____

Pays attention to story/activity: 5 minutes or less _____ 5–10 minutes _____ 10 minutes or longer _____

Concentrates on and completes a teacher-directed activity: most of the time _____ sometimes _____ rarely _____

Perseveres with a self-selected activity: most of the time _____ sometimes _____ rarely _____

Solves conflicts with other children: physically _____ with words _____ independently _____ with assistance _____

Follows directions the first time: frequently _____ sometimes _____ rarely _____

Follows two-step directions: frequently _____ sometimes _____ rarely _____

Please describe any particular strategies or accommodations that work well for this child:

_____

_____

Academic Readiness Abilities

Identifies letters: all _____ many _____ few _____ none _____ don't know _____

Knows letter sounds: all _____ many _____ few _____ none _____ don't know _____

Writes the alphabet: all _____ many _____ few _____ none _____ don't know _____

Writes his/her name: yes _____ no _____

Shows developmentally appropriate fine motor skills: yes _____ no _____

Counts: to 5 _____ to 10 _____ higher than 10 _____ not at all _____

Recognizes numbers 1–10: all _____ many _____ few _____ none _____

Writes letters: all _____ many _____ few _____ none _____

Writes numbers: a few _____ to 5 _____ to 10 or more _____ none _____

Can read: yes _____ no _____ don't know _____

Uses complete sentences to communicate in English: most of the time _____ some-times _____ rarely _____

Uses complete sentences to communicate in other language (_____): most of the time _____ sometimes _____ rarely _____

Language(s) this child speaks:

At home _____

At school _____

Does this child have an Individualized Education Program (IEP)? yes _____ no _____ don't know _____

Are there any support services that you know of that this child has received? _____
_____

Is there anything else you believe the kindergarten teachers need to know about this child? Please add any comments or concerns that would assist us in placing this child in the optimal classroom environment. Please use the back if necessary.

_____

_____

What is your overall opinion of this child's readiness for kindergarten?

definitely ready _____ somewhat ready _____ hopefully will be ready by fall _____
not at all ready _____

This student should be separated from the following students:

_____

_____

Remember, this form is *confidential!*
Thank you!

Teacher signature:

Date: _____

Resource 9.3 Family Survey—Letter of Introduction

Dear family,

Congratulations! Your child will be entering kindergarten this upcoming fall at _____ School. We are so excited to welcome you and your child to _____ School. In order to provide our kindergarten teaching faculty with more information about your child, we are asking you to please complete this questionnaire. Please be as objective and honest as you can. We know that all children are very different, and children vary in their strengths and challenges. The information you provide on this form will help us create balanced classrooms so that we can be ready for *all* entering kindergartners and do the best that we can to ensure that they have a happy and smooth start to school.

Please return this form to the _____ School office by June 1, 20__.

Many thanks,

_____

Principal, _____ School

Resource 9.4 Family Survey: Questions About Your Entering Kindergartner

Child's name: _____

Child's age today: years _____ months _____

Has your child attended a preschool program? yes _____ no _____

  Name of preschool: _____

  Number of years attended: _____

What are your child's favorite activities and favorite things to play?

What are your child's favorite things to do at home?

Where are your child's favorite places to go?

What are your child's strengths?

What things are most difficult for your child?

Circle the answer that best describes your child in each situation:

1. My child takes care of his/her personal needs such as cleaning up after him/herself, bathroom needs, and finding belongings.

   Almost never   Sometimes   Often   Almost always

2. My child generally approaches new activities and new situations . . .

   Enthusiastically   With some caution   Reluctantly

3. My child expresses and explains his/her ideas, feelings, and thoughts . . .

   Easily/Readily   Occasionally   Reluctantly/with caution   Never

4. My child forms new friendships easily.

   Almost never   Sometimes   Often   Almost always

(Continued)

(Continued)

5. My child pays attention to a story or attends to an activity for . . .

   5 minutes or less　　　*5 to 10 minutes*　　　*10 minutes or more*

6. How does your child handle difficult or challenging tasks?

   Tries hard to finish　　*Seeks help*　　*Shows frustration*　　*Gives up*

7. My child concentrates enough to finish a task or activity.

   Almost never　　*Sometimes*　　*Often*　　*Almost always*

8. My child remembers and follows directions without having them repeated.

   Almost never　　*Sometimes*　　*Often*　　*Almost always*

9. My child understands stories that he/she hears.

   Almost never　　*Sometimes*　　*Often*　　*Almost always*

10. My child knows the difference between *right* and *left*.

   Almost never　　*Sometimes*　　*Often*　　*Almost always*

11. My child knows the difference between *right* and *wrong*.

   Almost never　　*Sometimes*　　*Often*　　*Almost always*

12. My child can catch and throw a ball.

   Almost never　　*Sometimes*　　*Often*　　*Almost always*

13. My child demonstrates self-control.

   Almost never　　*Sometimes*　　*Often*　　*Almost always*

14. My child works out problems or conflicts with other children independently without force.

    Almost never   *Sometimes*   *Often*   *Almost always*

Circle all that apply:

15. My child likes to:

    Draw pictures

    Use scissors, glue sticks, markers

    Make puzzles

    Build with Legos

    Build with large blocks

    Work on the computer

    Write letters, words, and numbers

    Look at books

16. Early math skills:

    My child:

    Cannot count, recognize, or write the numbers to 5

    Can count, recognize, and write numbers to 5

    Can count, recognize, and write numbers to 10 or above

17. Early literacy skills:

    My child:

    Knows the letters of the alphabet

    Knows the letter sounds

    Can read some simple sight words

    Can read simple sentences

    Likes to read and look at books independently

    Likes to be read aloud to

Resource 9.5 Sample Letter to Families About Summer Kindergarten Readiness Program

Date:

Dear families,

Welcome to Kindergarten Readiness at _____ School! I am very excited to welcome you and your child to this exciting program. I would like to give you some information about what we will be doing, what your child will need to bring, and what our goals are for this week.

Please drop off your child at _____ (time) in front of Room _____ each day. Although I encourage you to walk your child into class, I will try my best to engage your child in an activity right away to make the separation from you smooth and painless! At the end of our day, we will bring the children outside the door at _____ (time) to have them meet you again. Please have your child dress in comfortable clothes with closed shoes appropriate for the playground (no crocs or sandals). Pack your child a substantially large, healthy (we have a no-sugar policy) snack and drink each day (even if you think your child will not be hungry—it is part of our routine). Please inform me as to whether your child has any food allergies or restrictions of any kind or takes any medications.

The primary goal of this program is to provide your child with a smooth transition process into kindergarten. Your child will be introduced to many routines, materials, and activities that he or she will encounter in kindergarten. Understanding daily routines, class rules and transitions, playing, sharing, working cooperatively with other children, and learning to be a good listener and active participant will be encouraged. Additionally, all these activities will help ensure a smooth and successful start to kindergarten in the fall.

All children enter kindergarten with great variability in their skills and abilities. Readiness for school is the composite of many factors and characteristics unique to each child. We will not be focusing on any particular skill or ability, but we will try to create a fun and positive classroom environment that your child looks forward to coming to each day and feels prepared for what to expect when kindergarten begins.

The underlying theme of this week will be _____! Through this hands-on, exploratory unit, your child will be introduced to _____ discovery, and _____. There will be many opportunities for reading, writing, listening, and speaking to develop early literacy skills, a love for reading, and a love for learning.

I have taught kindergarten at _____ School since _____ (year). I received my _____ (degree[s]) in education from _____ (university). I am pleased to have _____ (name) working with me. She is an instructional assistant in kindergarten at _____ School, and we have worked together for many years. I am also happy to introduce _____ (name), who will be part of our learning community each day, as well. Together, we will create a supportive and nurturing environment that will encourage cooperation, caring, respect, curiosity, sharing, and of course, readiness for kindergarten.

Please do not hesitate to contact me if you have any questions or concerns. You can reach me by e-mail at _____ (e-mail address) or by phone at _____ (personal or school phone). I will do everything I can to make this a memorable and successful program for you and your child.

Signed,

_____

Resource 9.6 Family Questionnaire From the New Kindergarten Teacher

- Student name:
- Name I would like my child to be called in class:
- Name I would like my child to learn to write in class:
- Any food or other allergies my child has:
- Parent name:
- Parent cell phone:
- Parent home phone:
- Parent work phone:
- E-mail address for contact information:
- Emergency contact:
- Second parent name:
- Parent cell phone:
- Parent home phone:
- Parent work phone:
- E-mail address for contact information:
- Emergency contact:

1. Describe several of your child's strengths and abilities.

2. Describe several of your child's difficulties or challenges.

3. What chores or responsibilities does your child have at home?

4. What kinds of things does your child like to do with you and your family?

5. What are your aspirations for your child and expectations for this year in school?

6. Do you have any special interests, hobbies, or skills you might like to share with the class?

Resource 9.7 Transitional Kindergarten

California was one of only four states in the country that admitted children to kindergarten before they were five years old. Children were required to turn five by December 2 of their kindergarten year. Senate Bill 1381 (Kindergarten Readiness Act of 2010, Simitian, Chapter 705) changed the kindergarten entry age in California from five years old by December 2 to five years old by September 1 so that children enter kindergarten at age 5. This new age requirement was designed to be phased in over three years, beginning in the 2012–13 school year. Those "young fives" (children turning five from September 2 to December 2) would then be eligible for *transitional kindergarten,* the first of a two-year kindergarten program designed specifically for these children. This new bill, passed and signed into law in September 2010, promises families (at no cost to them) the option of having their children in a classroom setting that uses a modified kindergarten curriculum that is age- and developmentally appropriate and will meet the educational as well as social and emotional needs of "young" five-year-olds. Transitional kindergarten (TK) was designed to better prepare children for success in kindergarten and beyond.

TK offers a bridge between preschool and kindergarten, providing a continuum of learning between the California's Preschool Learning Foundations and California Preschool Curriculum Frameworks, California Academic Content Standards for Kindergarten, and the Kindergarten Common Core State Standards for English Language Arts and Mathematics. Senate Bill 1381 requires that every district in California provide a TK program on school sites for any child displaced by the new entry date.

In a hands-on interactive classroom environment taught by credentialed K–12 teachers, the developmentally appropriate TK curriculum is delivered with an emphasis on exposure, exploration, and engagement rather than on mastery. The curriculum is comprehensive and balanced between all domains of early learning, with ample time devoted to further developing the social and emotional abilities children need for kindergarten. There is an emphasis on oral language development, communication skills, English language development, and self-regulation skills. Preschool California claims that TK addresses issues of social justice and equity by providing this additional and necessary year of developmentally appropriate learning experiences for children, leveling the field for all children, particularly those who experience an *opportunity gap*—lacking the benefit of a quality preschool or Head Start experience. Constructive play, intentional teaching, and a curriculum that supports all learning needs of young five-year-olds, blending the best practices of early childhood education with kindergarten, will become an integral part of the California K–12 system.

The California Kindergarten Association has advocated for this age change for over 30 years. This landmark legislation will ensure that all children are ready to learn, are prepared for the rigor of kindergarten, and will be successful in kindergarten and beyond. TK will also most likely save the state money from reduced rates of retention, intervention, and special education placement.

Some districts have already begun early implementation of TK in their schools. Some schools have designed combination (*combo*) classes of pre-K/TK, TK/K, or "pure" TK classrooms. The next few years to come are exciting ones as we see if the desired results of TK are being achieved!

TK Schedule Sample A (Half Day)

8:15 Students arrive

8:15–8:30 Welcome/Morning Message/Calendar

8:30–9:15 Learning Center Rotations: Math Exploration; Language Arts (independent reading, guided reading groups, buddy reading, writing centers, phonemic awareness, phonics, alphabet writing/work); Science; Social Studies

9:15–9:30 Read Aloud/Shared Reading

9:30–10:00 Recess/Snack

10:00–10:30 Choice Time (building center, discovery center, writing center, dramatic play center, art center, technology)

10:30–11:00 Art, Music, Movement, or PE

11:00–11:15 Early Literacy (whole group)

11:15–11:20 Clean Up

11:20–11:30 Class Meeting (community circle)

11:30 Dismissal

TK Schedule Sample B (Full Day)

8:15 Students arrive

8:15–8:30 Welcome/Morning Message/Calendar

8:30–9:30 Early Literacy

9:30–9:45 Oral Language Development and Language Arts

9:45–10:05 Recess

10:05–10:35 Math Centers

10:35–11:15 Music, Movement, or PE/Art

11:15–12:00 Lunch and Recess

12:00–1:00 Learning Center Rotations: Math Exploration, Language Arts (independent reading, guided reading groups, buddy reading, writing centers, phonemic awareness, phonics, alphabet writing/work)

1:00–1:30 Choice Time/Outdoor Interest Areas

1:30–1:35 Clean Up

1:35–2:00 Writer's Workshop: Emergent Writing

2:00–2:15 Author's Chair: Sharing Writing

2:15–2:25 Class Meeting (community circle)

2:30 Dismissal

Sources: Kindergarten Readiness Act of 2010, SB 1381, 2010 California State Legislation; Preschool California (www.preschoolcalifornia.org); California Kindergarten Association (www.californiakindergartenassociation.org).

PROFESSIONAL DEVELOPMENT DISCUSSION GUIDE

1. Deepen Your Thinking:
   a. Choose one or more of these individual inquiry topics for group discussion:
      i. What are one or two transition practices your school currently is not involved in that you believe you can begin to implement during this or the next school year? Why are they particularly important to you?
      ii. How will you communicate the importance of transition practices to your community?
      iii. Using only one of the 13 transition practices listed, brainstorm how you would go about implementing this new practice.

WHERE CAN I LEARN MORE?

California Kindergarten Association
http://www.californiakindergartenassociation.org

First 5 California http://www.ccfc.ca.gov/

Kindergarten in California (California Department of Education)
http://www.cde.ca.gov/ci/gs/em/kinderinfo.asp

Kindergarten Readiness Act of 2010, SB 1381, 2010 State Legislature
http://www.leginfo.ca.cov/pub/09-10/bill/sen/sb_1351-1400/sb_1381_bill_20100930_chaptered.html

Preschool California http://www.preschoolcalifornia.org

Preschool California: Transitional Kindergarten Library http://www.tkcalifornia.org

Preschool Curriculum Framework, Volume 1
http://www.cde.ca.gov/sp/cd/re/documents/psframeworkkvol1.pdf

Preschool Learning Foundations, Volume 1
http://www.cde.ca.gov/sp/cd/re/documents/preschoollf.pdf

Transitional Kindergarten Frequently Asked Questions
http://www.cde.ca.gov/ci/gs/em/kinderfaq.asp

10 Conclusion

R eadiness for school has become a growing concern in this country. Entering kindergartners begin school with considerable variation in their range of general knowledge, skills, and abilities. They come from increasingly diverse ethnic, racial, cultural, social, economic, and language backgrounds, and they differ in the types of early care and educational experiences prior to kindergarten (West, Denton, & Germino Hausken, 2000; West, Denton, & Reaney, 2001; Zill & West, 2001). Many children begin school unprepared for the increasing demands of kindergarten. Kindergarten readiness has received increased attention from parents, educators, researchers, and legislators, who together promote efforts to raise the quality of early learning programs to facilitate children's better preparation for school success.

Recent conceptualizations of readiness articulate the inclusion of families, schools, and communities. It has been suggested that understanding the interrelationship among parenting, the home-school partnership, and the teacher-child relationship is more effective than concentrating on isolated skills and abilities solely within the child (Ponitz, McClelland, Matthews, & Morrison, 2009). Scott-Little et al. (Scott-Little, Kagan, & Frelow, 2003a, 2003b, 2005, 2006; Scott-Little, Lesko, Martella, & Milburn, 2007) claimed that dialogue among these stakeholders is necessary for effective implementation, because each group of stakeholders makes an important contribution to articulating conceptualizations of readiness and brings a unique perspective of what is important for children's readiness for school.

Past studies have indicated that many children enter kindergarten at risk for school failure (West et al., 2000; West et al., 2001; Zill & West, 2001); kindergarten teachers have reported that more than half of children enter school with a number of problems, such as not following directions and not being able to work independently (Pianta, Cox, Taylor, & Early, 1999; Rimm-Kaufman, Pianta, & Cox, 2000), and that a significant number of children enter kindergarten not optimally ready to learn (Hains, Fowler, Schwartz, Kottwitz, & Rosenkoetter, 1989; Piotrkowski, Botsko, & Matthews, 2000). These problems have significant implications for the shifting academic expectations that children face from preschool to kindergarten and the expectations that kindergarten teachers have for incoming students. Common themes that also emerged from these past studies included kindergarten teachers' perceptions that social and emotional development, overall physical health, and positive approaches toward learning (rather than purely academic development) are critical precursors of kindergarten readiness. Contrary to kindergarten teachers' beliefs, the states have placed a strong emphasis on language, literacy, cognition, and general knowledge in their early learning standards. Recent research supports not only healthy development in all areas of early learning and development but the availability of high-quality, developmentally appropriate preschool education to support young children's growth and development.

The theoretical framework of this book, grounded in the work of the National Education Goals Panel (NEGP; Kagan, Moore, & Bredekamp, 1995), conceptualizes readiness as a multidimensional model that incorporates the interrelatedness of families, early childhood education programs, schools, teachers, and the broader community to support children's early learning and development. The particular skills, abilities, characteristics, and knowledge that each individual child brings to school are a function of both the readiness of the child's environment before beginning kindergarten and the readiness of the schools in which they enroll (Copple, 1997; Kagan et al., 1995; NAEYC, 2004; NEGP, 1997; Shore, 1998).

This book suggests that greater attention should be paid to a broader, more integrated nurturing of children's development during the preschool years, with exposure to learning experiences in *all* constructs. Kindergarten benchmarks should be established so that certain important academic abilities are recognized as *exit* skills, not *entry* skills. Kindergarten students should be given the opportunity to continue to grow in all areas of early learning and development during the kindergarten year without being expected to perform isolated tasks measuring their cognitive and literacy abilities to the exclusion of recognizing and encouraging growth in other areas. With the availability of early learning standards that reflect a more balanced approach with an emphasis on *all* domains of early learning and development; with effective transition practices among preschool, home, and kindergarten; and with greater attention paid to the ways in which kindergarten teachers perceive readiness, *all* children in this country will enter kindergarten more prepared for the rigorous curriculum and standards they face, and schools and teachers will show readiness for *all* entering kindergartners.

The author is hopeful that this book can do the following: help bridge the gap between preschool and kindergarten; help strengthen the communication and collaboration between instructional practices in preschools and kindergarten; provide consistency among the expectations that kindergarten teachers, preschool teachers, and families hold about readiness; and encourage transition practices that will help facilitate the move and adjustment to kindergarten so that children start school ready to learn.

Readiness must be conceptualized as a broad construct that incorporates all aspects of a child's life that contribute directly to that child's ability to learn. Definitions of readiness must take into account the environment, context, and conditions under which the child acquires skills and is encouraged to learn. Assessments of readiness must, in consequence, incorporate data collected over time from the child, teacher, parents, and community. In short, these thoughts help us restate the first national goal as follows:

> By the year 2000, all children will have an opportunity to enhance their skills, knowledge, and abilities by participating in classrooms that are sensitive to community values, recognize individual differences, reinforce and extend children's strengths, and assist them in overcoming their difficulties. (Meisels, 1999, pp. 62–63)

References

American Psychiatric Association. (2000). *Diagnostic and statistical manual of mental disorders: DSM-IV-TR*. Washington, DC: Author.

Appl, D. J., & Pratt, T. (2007). Children's books as a vehicle for teaching teachers ways to help children value differences. *Young Exceptional Children, 10*(4), 2–10.

Armstrong, T. (1994). *Multiple intelligences in the classroom*. Alexandria, VA: Association for Supervision and Curriculum Development.

Barnett, W. S., Epstein, D. J., Carolan, M. E., Fitzgerald, J., Ackerman, D. J., & Friedman, A. H. (2010). *The state of preschool: 2010 state preschool yearbook*. New Brunswick, NJ: NIEER.

Barnett, W. S., Epstein, D. J., Friedman, A. H., Boyd, J. S., & Hustedt, J. T. (2008). *The state of preschool: 2008 state preschool yearbook*. New Brunswick, NJ: NIEER.

Barnett, W. S., & Yarosz, D. J. (2007). Who goes to preschool and why does it matter: Preschool policy matters. New Brunswick, NJ: National Institute for Early Education Research.

Biemiller, A. (2001, Spring). Teaching vocabulary: Early, direct, and sequential. *American Educator, 25*(1), 24-28, 47.

Biemiller, A. (2003, Spring). Oral comprehension sets the ceiling on reading comprehension. *American Educator, 27*, 23-44.

Bowman, B. T., Donovan, M. S., & Burns, M. S. (Eds.). (2001). *Eager to learn: Educating our preschoolers*. Washington, DC: National Academy Press.

Boyd, J., Barnett, W. S., Bodrova, E., Leong, D. J., & Gomby, D. (2005). Promoting children's social and emotional development though preschool education. New Brunswick, NJ: National Institute for Early Education Research.

Cappelloni, N. L. (2011). *Reading standards for literature: Key ideas and details*. Retrieved from California Kindergarten Association website: http://www.californiakindergartenassociation.org/2011/10/20/october-common-core-state-standards-lessons/

Cappelloni, Nancy L. (2010). *Kindergarten teachers' perceptions of kindergarten readiness*. (Doctoral dissertation). Retrieved from *Dissertation Abstracts International* (DAI).

Cappelloni, N., & Niesyn, M. (2007). *Teaching conflict resolution in the primary school classroom through children's literature*. (Doctoral paper). San Francisco, CA: University of San Francisco, School of Education, S.F.

Children and Adults with Attention Deficit/Hyperactivity Disorder (CHADD). (2012). *Understanding ADHD: What are the symptoms of ADHD?* Retrieved February 1, 2010, from http://www.chadd.org/Content/CHADD/Understanding/Symptoms/default.htm

Christenson, S. L. (1999). Families and schools: Rights, responsibilities, resources, and relationships. In R. C. Pianta & M. J. Cox (Eds.), *The transition to kindergarten* (pp. 143–177). Baltimore, MD: Paul H. Brookes.

Collins A., Brown, J. S., & Holum, A. (1991, Winter). Cognitive apprenticeship: Making thinking visible. *American Educator, 6*(11), 38–46.

Collins, L. (2002). Teaching conflict resolution through literature. *Delta Kappa Gamma Bulletin, 69*(1), 15–18.

Common Core State Standards Initiative. (2011). Retrieved January 6, 2012, from http://www.corestandards.org/the-standards/english-language-arts-standards; http://www.corestandards.org/the-standards/mathematics

Copple, C. (1997). Getting a good start in school. *National Education Goals Panel.* Washington, DC: US Government Printing Office.

Copple, C., & Bredekamp, S. (Eds.). (2009). *Developmentally appropriate practice in early childhood programs.* Washington, DC: National Association for the Education of Young Children.

Daggett, W. (2008). Ensuring access through differentiated instruction. *The Special Edge, Summer,* 3–4.

Darling-Hammond, L., Bransford, J., Featherstone, H., Feiman-Nemser, S., Kirsch, E., Lovelace-Taylor, K., . . . Sparks, D. (2009). *The learning classroom: Theory into practice* [print guide]. Detroit, MI: Annenberg Foundation. Available from http://www.learner.org/resources/series172.html

Denton, K., & West, J. (2002). *Children's reading and mathematics achievement in kindergarten and first grade* (NCES 2001–125). Washington, DC: National Center for Education Statistics, U.S. Department of Education.

Domitrovich, C. E., Gest, S. D., Gill, S., Bierman, K. L., Welsh, J. A., & Jones, D. (2009). Fostering high-quality teaching with an enriched curriculum and professional development support: The Head Start REDI program. *American Educational Research Journal, 46,* 567–597.

DuFour, R. (2004). Schools as learning communities. *Association for Supervision and Curriculum Development (ASCD), 61*(8), 6–11.

Early, D. M., Pianta, R. C., Taylor, L. C., & Cox, M. J. (2001). Transition practices: Findings from a national survey of kindergarten teachers. *Early Childhood Education Journal, 28,* 199–206.

Easton, L. B. (2011). Professional development discussion guide. *Phi Delta Kappan, 93*(4), 1–14.

Fantuzzo, J. W., King, J. A., & Heller, L. R. (1992). Effects of reciprocal peer tutoring on mathematics and school adjustment: A component analysis. *Journal of Educational Psychology, 84,* 331–339.

Feeney, S., & Moravcik, E. (2005). Children's literature: A window to understanding self and others. *Young Children, 60*(5), 20–28.

Gesell Institute of Child Development. (2011). *Gesell developmental observation-revised examiner's manual.* New Haven, CT: Author. Available at http://www.gesellinstitute.org/GDO-R_Overview_Document.html

Hains, A. H., Fowler, S. A., Schwartz, I. S., Kottwitz, E., & Rosenkoetter, S. (1989). A comparison of preschool and kindergarten teacher expectations for school readiness. *Early Childhood Research Quarterly, 4,* 75–88.

Hair, E., Halle, T., Terry-Humen, E., Lavelle, B., & Calkins, J. (2006). Children's school readiness in the ECLS-K: Predictions to academic, health, and social outcomes in first grade. *Early Childhood Research Quarterly, 21,* 431–454.

Hamre, B. K., & Pianta, R. C. (2007). Learning opportunities in preschool and early elementary classrooms. In R. C. Pianta, M. J. Cox, & K. L. Snow (Eds.), *School readiness and the transition to kindergarten in the era of accountability* (pp. 49–83). Baltimore, MD: Paul H. Brookes.

Hart, B., & Risley, T. R. (1995). *Meaningful differences in the everyday experience of young American children.* Baltimore, MD: Paul H. Brookes.

Hart, B., & Risley, T. R. (2003, Spring). The early catastrophe: The 30 million word gap by age 3. *American Educator.* Retrieved April 8, 2008, from http://www .aft.org/pubs-reports/american_educator/spring2003/catastrophe.html

Head Start Bureau. (2005). *Head start impact study: First year findings.* Washington, DC: U.S. Department of Health and Human Services. Retrieved April 15, 2009, from http://www.acf.hhs.gov/programs/opre/hs/impact_study/index.html

Heaviside, S., & Farris, E. (1993). *Public school teachers' views on children's readiness for school* (NCES 93–410). Washington, DC: National Center for Education Statistics, U.S. Department of Education.

Iruka, I. U., & Carver, P. R. (2006). *National household education surveys program of 2005* (NCES 2006–075). Washington, DC: National Center for Education Statistics, U.S. Department of Education.

Jonson, K., Cappelloni, N., & Niesyn, M. (2011). *The new elementary teacher's handbook* (3rd ed.). Thousand Oaks, CA: Corwin.

Kagan, S. L., Carroll, J., Comer, J. P., & Scott-Little, C. (2006). Alignment: A missing link in early childhood transitions? *Young Children, 61,* 26–32.

Kagan, S. L., Moore, E., & Bredekamp, S. (Eds.). (1995*). Reconsidering children's early development and learning: Toward common views and vocabulary* (Report of the National Education Goals Panel, Goal 1 Technical Planning Group). Washington, DC: U.S. Government Printing Office.

Kemple, D. M., David, G. M., & Hysmith, C. (1997). Teachers' interventions in preschool and kindergarten children's peer interactions. *Journal of Research in Childhood Education, 12,* 34–47.

Kindergarten Readiness Act of 2010, SB 1381, 2010 State Legislature. (2010). http://www.leginfo.ca.cov/pub/09–10/bill/sen/sb_13511400/sb_1381_bill_20100930_chaptered.html

LaParo, K. M., & Pianta, R. C. (2000). Predicting children's competence in the early school years: A meta-analytic review. *Review of Educational Research, 70,* 443–484.

Lemerise, E. A., & Arsenio, W. F. (2000). An integrated model of emotion processes and cognition in social information processing. *Child Development, 71*(1), 107–118.

Lin, H., Lawrence, F. R., & Gorrell, J. (2003). Kindergarten teachers' views of children's readiness for school. *Early Childhood Research Quarterly, 18,* 225–237.

LoCasale-Crouch, J., Mashburn, A. J., Downer, J. T., & Pianta, R. C. (2008). Prekindergarten teachers' use of transition practices and children's adjustment to kindergarten. *Early Childhood Research Quarterly, 23,* 124–139.

Logue, M. E. (2007). Early childhood learning standards: Tools for promoting social and academic success in kindergarten. *Children and Schools, 29,* 35–43.

Lonigan, C. J., Burgess, S. R., & Anthony, J. L. (2000). Development of emergent literacy and early reading skills in preschool children: Evidence from a latent-variable longitudinal study. *Developmental Psychology, 36,* 596–613.

Lubliner, S., & Smetana, L. (2005). *Getting into words: Vocabulary instruction that strengthens comprehension.* Baltimore, MD: Paul H. Brookes.

Lunenburg, F. C. (2000). Early childhood education programs can make a difference in academic, economic, and social arenas. *Education, 120,* 519–528.

Magnuson, K. A., Ruhm, C., & Waldfogel, J. (2007). Does prekindergarten improve school preparation and performance? *Economics of Education Review, 25*, 33–51.

Marcon, R. A. (2002). Moving up the grades: Relationship between preschool model and later school success. *Early Childhood Research and Practice, 4*(1). Retrieved March 23, 2009, from http://ecrp.uiuc.edu/v4n1/marcon.html

Marin County Office of Education (MCOE), Department of Special Education, California. (2011). Retrieved February 15, 2012, from http://jade .marinschools.org/Student-Programs/Special-Education/Pages/Early-Start.aspx

Marin County Office of Education (MCOE), Special Education, Early Intervention. (2011). Retrieved February 15, 2012, from http://jade.marinschools.org/ Student-Programs/Special Education/Pages/Early- Intervention.aspx

Mashburn, A. J. (2008). Quality of social and physical environments in preschools and children's development of academic, language, and literacy skills. *Applied Developmental Science, 12*, 113–127.

McCabe, L. A., & Frede, E. C. (2007). Challenging behaviors and the role of preschool education. New Brunswick, NJ: National Institute for Early Education Research.

McClelland, M. M., Acock, A. C., & Morrison, F. J. (2006). The impact of kindergarten learning-related skills on academic trajectories at the end of elementary school. *Early Childhood Research Quarterly, 21*, 471–490.

Meisels, S. J. (1999). Assessing readiness. In R. C. Pianta & M. J. Cox (Eds.), *The transition to kindergarten* (pp. 39–66). Baltimore, MD: Paul H. Brookes.

Montie, J. E., Xiang, Z., & Schweinhart, L. J. (2006). Preschool experience in 10 countries: Cognitive and language performance at age 7. *Early Childhood Research Quarterly, 21*, 313–331.

National Association for the Education of Young Children (NAEYC). (2004). *Where we stand on school readiness.* Washington, DC: NAEYC.

National Association for the Education of Young Children (NAEYC). (2009). *Developmentally appropriate practice in early childhood programs serving children from birth through age 8.* Washington, DC: NAEYC. Retrieved January 3, 2012, from http://NAEYC.org

National Association for the Education of Young Children and National Association of Early Childhood Specialists in State Departments of Education (NAEYC & NAECS/SDE). (2002). *Early learning standards.* Washington, DC: NAEYC.

National Center for Children in Poverty (NCCP). (2012). *Basic facts about low-income children, birth to age 6.* Retrieved February 23, 2012, from http://www .nccp.org/publications/pub_1054.html

National Center for Education Statistics. (2012). *Early childhood longitudinal study: Kindergarten class of 2010–2011.* Retrieved March 11, 2012, from http://nces .ed.gov/ecls/myeclsk2011/index.asp

National Education Goals Panel. (1993). *Background on the National Education Goals Panel.* Retrieved January 9, 2010, from http://www.ed.gov/pubs/goals/ report/goalsrpt.txt

National Education Goals Panel. (1997). *Special early childhood report.* Washington, DC: National Institute for Literacy.

National Institute for Literacy. (2009). Developing early literacy: Report of the National Early Literacy Panel: A scientific synthesis of early literacy development and implications for intervention. *National Center for Family Literacy.* Retrieved February 15, 2012, from http://lincs.ed.gov/publications/pdf/NELPReport09.pdf

Neuman, S. B., & Cunningham, L. (2009). The impact of professional development and coaching on early language and literacy instructional practices. *American Educational Research Journal, 46*, 532–566.

O'Donnell, K. (2008). *Parents' reports of the school readiness of young children from the national household education surveys program of 2007* (NCES 2008–051). Washington, DC: National Center for Education Statistics, Institute of Education Sciences, U.S. Department of Education.

Pace, R., & Podesta, A. (1999). Teaching peace with Dr. Seuss. *Kappa Delta Pi Record, 35*(3), 118–121.

Pajares, M. F. (1992). Teachers' beliefs and educational research: Cleaning up a messy construct. *Review of Educational Research, 62*, 307–332.

Palmer, J. (2001). Conflict resolution: Strategies for the elementary classroom. *Early Childhood Education 28*(1), 65–68.

Pearson Early Childhood Assessments. (2012). *Pearson Early Childhood Assessments.* San Antonio, TX: Pearson Clinical Assessment.

Perry, N. E., & VandeKamp, K. J. O. (2000). Creating classroom contexts that support young children's development of self-regulated learning. *International Journal of Educational Research, 33*, 821–843.

Perry, N. E., VandeKamp, K. O., Mercer, L. K., & Nordby, C. J. (2002). Investigating teacher-student interactions that foster self-regulated learning. *Educational Psychologist, 37*, 5–15.

Pianta, R. C., & Cox, M. J. (1999). The changing nature of the transition to school: Trends for the next decade. In R. C. Pianta & M. J. Cox (Eds.), *The transition to kindergarten* (pp. 363–379). Baltimore, MD: Paul H. Brookes.

Pianta, R.C., Cox, M. J., Taylor, L., & Early, D. (1999). Kindergarten teachers; practices related to the transition to school: Results of a national survey. *The Elementary School Journal, 100*, 71–86.

Pianta, R. C., & Howes, C. (2009). *The promise of Pre-K.* Baltimore, MD: Paul H. Brookes.

Piotrkowski, C. S., Botsko, M., & Matthews, E. (2000). Parents' and teachers' beliefs about children's school readiness in a high-need community. *Early Childhood Research Quarterly, 15*, 537–558.

Ponitz, C. C., McClelland, M. M., Matthews, J. S., & Morrison, F. J. (2009). A structured observation of behavioral self-regulation and its contribution to kindergarten outcomes. *Developmental Psychology, 45*, 605–619.

Princiotta, D., Flanagan, K. D., & Germino Hausken, E. (2006). *Fifth grade: Findings from the fifth-grade follow-up of the Early Childhood Longitudinal Study, Kindergarten Class of 1998–99 (ECLS-K)* (NCES 2006–038). Washington, DC: National Center for Education Statistics, U.S. Department of Education.

Rimm-Kaufman, S. E., Pianta, R. C., & Cox, M. J. (2000). Teachers' judgments of problems in the transition to kindergarten. *Early Childhood Research Quarterly, 15*, 147–166.

Scott-Little, C., Kagan, S. L., & Frelow, V. S. (2003a). Creating the conditions for success with early learning standards: Results from a national study of state-level standards for children's learning prior to kindergarten. *Early Childhood Research and Practice, 5*(2). Retrieved February 19, 2009, from http://ecrp.uiuc.edu/v5n2/little.html

Scott-Little, C., Kagan, S. L., & Frelow, V. S. (2003b). *Standards for preschool children's learning and development: Who has standards, how were they developed, and how are they used?* Greensboro, NC: SERVE. Retrieved January 19, 2009, from http://www.serve.org/TT/Early%20Learning%20Standards.pdf

Scott-Little, C., Kagan, S. L., & Frelow, V. S. (2005). *Inside the content: The depth and breadth of early learning standards.* Greensboro, NC: SERVE. Retrieved January 19, 2009, from http://www.serve.org/_downloads/publications/insidecontentfr.pdf

Scott-Little, C., Kagan, S. L., & Frelow, V. S. (2006). Conceptualization of readiness and the content of early learning standards: The intersection of policy and research? *Early Childhood Research and Practice, 21,* 153–173.

Scott-Little, C., Lesko, J., Martella, J., & Milburn, P. (2007). Early learning standards: Results from a national survey to document trends in state-level policies and practices. *Early Childhood Research and Practice, 9*(1). Retrieved March 19, 2009, from http://ecrp.uic.edu/v9n1/little.html

Shannon, S. M. (2007). *Please don't label my child: Break the doctor-diagnosis-drug cycle and discover safe, effective choices for your child's emotional health.* New York, NY: Rodale.

Shonkoff, J. P, & Phillips, D. A. (Eds.). (2000). *From neurons to neighborhoods: The science of early childhood development.* Washington, DC: National Academy Press.

Shore, R. (1998). *Ready schools* (Report of the National Education Goals Panel, Goal 1 Technical Planning Group). Washington, DC: U.S. Government Printing Office.

Singer, D. G., & Revenson, T. A. (1996). *A Piaget primer: How a child thinks.* New York, NY: Penguin Books.

Snider, V. E., & Roehl, R. (2007). Teachers' beliefs about pedagogy and related issues. *Psychology in the Schools, 44,* 873–886.

Snow, C., Burns, S, & Griffin, P. (Eds.). (1998). *Preventing reading difficulties in young children.* Washington, DC: National Academy Press.

Snow, K. (2011). *Developing kindergarten readiness and other large-scale assessment systems: Necessary considerations in the assessment of young children.* Washington, DC: National Association for the Education of Young Children.

Snyder, T. D., Dillow, S. A., & Hoffman, C. M. (2008). *Digest of education statistics 2007* (NCES 2008–022). Washington, DC: National Center for Education Statistics, Institute of Education Sciences, U.S. Department of Education.

Strickland, D. S., & Riley-Ayers, S. (2006). *Early literacy: Policy and practice in the preschool years.* New Brunswick, NJ: NIEER.

Thompson, R.A. (2008). *Connecting neurons, concepts, and people: Brain development and its implications.* New Brunswick, NJ: NIEER.

Tremblay, R. E., Gervais, J., & Petitclerc, A. (2008). *Early learning prevents youth violence.* (Report by the Centre of Excellence for Early Childhood Development). Montreal, Quebec: Canadian Council on Learning. http://www.excellence-earlychildhood.ca/documents/Tremblay_AggressionReport_ANG.pdf

U.S. Department of Education, Individuals with Disabilities Education Act (IDEA). (2004). Retrieved on February 12, 2012, from http://idea.ed.gov

Vygotsky, L. S. (1978). *Mind in society: The development of higher psychological processes.* Cambridge, MA: Harvard University Press.

Walston, J., Rathbun, A., & Germino Hausken, E. (2008). *Eighth grade: First findings from the final round of the early childhood longitudinal study, kindergarten class of*

1998–99 (ECLS-K) (NCES 2008–088). Washington, DC: National Center for Education Statistics, U.S. Department of Education.

Wesley, P. W., & Buysse, V. (2003). Making meaning of school readiness in schools and communities. *Early Childhood Research Quarterly, 18,* 351–375.

West, J., Denton, K., & Germino Hausken, E. (2000). *America's kindergartners: Findings from the early childhood longitudinal study, kindergarten class of 1998–99 (ECLS-K)* (NCES 2001–070R). Washington, DC: National Center for Education Statistics, U.S. Department of Education.

West, J., Denton, K., & Reaney, L. M. (2001). *The kindergarten year: Findings from the early childhood longitudinal study, kindergarten class of 1998–99 (ECLS-K)* (NCES 2001–023R). Washington, DC: National Center for Education Statistics, U.S. Department of Education.

Wolfgang, C. H., Stannard, L. L., & Jones, I. (2001). Block play performance among preschoolers as a predictor of later school achievement in mathematics. *Journal of Research in Childhood Education, 15,* 173–180.

Zill, N. (1999). Promoting educational equity and excellence in kindergarten. In R. C. Pianta & M. J. Cox (Eds.), *The transition to kindergarten* (pp. 67–105). Baltimore, MD: Paul H. Brookes.

Zill, N., & West, J. (2001). *Entering kindergarten: A portrait of American children when they begin school: Findings from the condition of education 2000* (NCES 2001–035). Washington, DC: National Center for Education Statistics, U.S. Department of Education.

Index

CORWIN
A SAGE Company

The Corwin logo—a raven striding across an open book—represents the union of courage and learning. Corwin is committed to improving education for all learners by publishing books and other professional development resources for those serving the field of PreK–12 education. By providing practical, hands-on materials, Corwin continues to carry out the promise of its motto: **"Helping Educators Do Their Work Better."**